T0351427

"You @ the U is like having an advisor in your back pocket ... I wish
I would have had a resource like this when I was starting out
on my academic career."
– ERIN LUONG, president, Alberta Teachers' Association,
Council of School Counsellors

"You @ the U is a great resource to help students navigate their first
year of postsecondary education. It is practical and grounded in
Dr. Miller's first-hand experiences working with university students for
many years. This step-by-step guide will save students a lot of stress!"
– ANUSHA KASSAN, associate professor, Department of Educational and Counselling
Psychology, and Special Education, University of British Columbia

"You @ the U empowers students to understand what to expect
and how to access support before they hit a wall!"
– CINDY MANCUSO, career counsellor/diversity advisor, McGill University

"Just like Dorothy in the Wizard of Oz, by the time you are finished
reading this book you'll realize that you already possess everything you
need to thrive on your unique postsecondary journey."
– NEIL BUDDEL, vice-president, Student Success, Centennial College

"What strikes me the most about this book is how down-to-earth and
practical it is. For example, I personally related to the part that showed
how a procrastinating student – who feels the demands of the semester
come crashing down – can still make effective decisions. Janet walks
the student through a decision-making process to find a path forward.
Will I continue to use this book with first-year students seeking to
find their way in the university? Simply put: Yes!"
– GLEN RYLAND, undergraduate studies coordinator, Mount Royal University

The ON CAMPUS imprint of UBC Press features publications designed for the diverse members of the university community – students, faculty, instructors, and administrators. ON CAMPUS offers a range of interesting, sometimes unconventional, but always useful information. All ON CAMPUS works are assessed by experts in the field prior to publication. To ensure ON CAMPUS materials are easily obtainable, they are made available for free download in digital format or for purchase in print.

Resources for students are designed to help them successfully meet the intellectual and social challenges encountered at university or college today. The inaugural book in the ON CAMPUS imprint was the highly successful *How to Succeed at University (and Get a Great Job!): Mastering the Critical Skills You Need for School, Work, and Life*, which is also available in French from University of Ottawa Press. The subsequent book was *It's All Good (Unless It's Not): Mental Health Tips and Self-Care Strategies for Your Undergrad Years*, by Nicole Malette.

To find out more about ON CAMPUS books visit www.ubcpress.ca or follow us on social media.

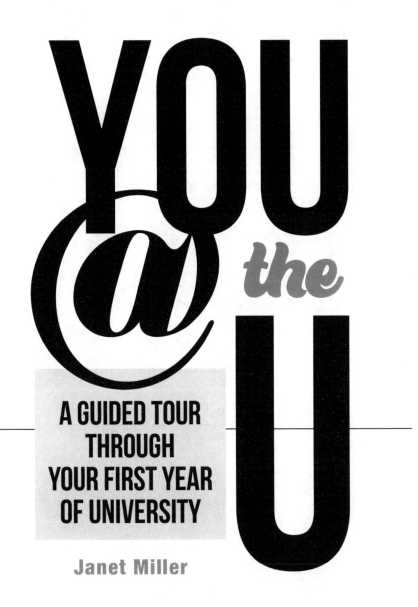

YOU @ the U

A GUIDED TOUR THROUGH YOUR FIRST YEAR OF UNIVERSITY

Janet Miller

UBC PRESS

It is my pleasure to dedicate this book to my family –
Hannah, Mark, Alex, Ben, and Randy.
I am so deeply grateful to share this life with you.

© 2021 On Campus, an imprint of UBC Press

All rights reserved. No part of this publication may be reproduced,
stored in a retrieval system, or transmitted, in any form or by any means, without
prior written permission of the publisher, or, in Canada, in the
case of photocopying or other reprographic copying, a licence from
Access Copyright, www.accesscopyright.ca.

30 29 28 27 26 25 24 23 22   5 4 3 2

Printed in Canada on FSC-certified ancient-forest-free paper
(100% postconsumer recycled) that is processed chlorine- and acid-free.

Library and Archives Canada Cataloguing in Publication

Title: You @ the U : a guided tour through your first year of university / Janet Miller.
Other titles: You at the U
Names: Miller, Janet (University counsellor), author.
Description: Includes bibliographical references and index.
Identifiers: Canadiana (print) 20210209240 | Canadiana (ebook) 20210209593
ISBN 9780774839051 (softcover) | ISBN 9780774839068 (PDF) | ISBN 9780774839075 (EPUB)
Subjects: LCSH: College freshmen – Life skills guides.
LCSH: College student orientation.
Classification: LCC LB2343.3 .M55 2021 | DDC 378.1/98—dc23

Canada

UBC Press gratefully acknowledges the financial support for our
publishing program of the Government of Canada (through the Canada Book Fund),
the Canada Council for the Arts, and the British Columbia Arts Council.

Printed and bound in Canada by Friesens
Set in Caecilia, Frontage, and Helvetica Neue by Gerilee McBride
Substantive and copy editor: Lesley Erickson
Proofreader: Carmen Tiampo
Indexer: Patricia Buchanan
Cover and interior designer: Gerilee McBride

UBC Press
The University of British Columbia
2029 West Mall
Vancouver, BC V6T 1Z2
www.ubcpress.ca

CONTENTS

BLESSINGS FOR ALL ON YOUR JOURNEY

WHEN WE ENTER an institution such as a university, it is difficult to enter strange terrain and navigate our way into a first day of class, especially when we come from out of town or a reserve, and sometimes, never having lived in a big city. Adjusting to a whole new environment is a daunting and fearful task, but trial and error in acclimating ourselves to a new environment slowly leads to newfound friends as well as getting us used to the layout of the university. But that is only the beginning of a journey that will take you through three to four years until graduation. It is indeed scary, but navigable with all the resources available to make a student's journey manageable. A book to read about expectations from people who have gone through this helps. A book to help new students overcome their fears and answer questions that they may have about university is always welcome.

This is my heartfelt blessing and is meant for to be for all new and continuing university students.

Land Acknowledgment

The Blackfoot land acknowledgment is often echoed during events related to the Traditional Territory of the Niitsi tapi, or the Real People, and this is what people in the audience often hear. An example is the land acknowledgment at Mount Royal University (www.mtroyal.ca), where Janet Miller works.

Mount Royal University is located in the Traditional Territories of the Niitsi tapi (Blackfoot) and the people of the Treaty 7 region in southern Alberta, which include the Siksika, the Piikani, the Kainai, the Tsuut'ina, and the Iyarhe Nakoda. The City of Calgary is also home to the Métis Nation.

There are many different versions of the land acknowledgment that we hear throughout the vast Blackfoot Traditional Territory. It is about paying respect to the people that inhabited the land long before contact. In order to begin the process of understanding it, we must go back and provide a "voice back to the land." We must turn our attention to pre-contact – to the signing of Treaty 7 – to the present, in order to further understand what this land acknowledgment really means, hence, "giving voice back to the land." Since time immemorial, the Blackfoot Traditional Territory has allowed many footprints to tread upon it, including hoof prints and claw prints because we share the land with the animals, which are also part and parcel of the land. Even the birds that fly around in the sky, those that live underneath the land, and those that live in the rivers too. Even the plants and trees that have their roots planted in the soil are part of the land. The land sustained the Blackfoot people in the form of food and medicine, and the land provided many other necessities of life for the Blackfoot people. The buffalo or *inii* (in Blackfoot) was welcomed into the territory so that the Blackfoot people could live off of it; it provided the village with food, clothing and shelter. The buffalo was a gift from the Creator.

Land acknowledgments are heard on the surface to pay homage and respect to the people that lived in a particular area before contact. In the past, Indigenous people's relationship with nature was one of respect based on the notion that we all are interrelated. Respecting nature brings about harmony that transcends into balance, which is reciprocal. It means that whatever harm people do to nature will affect them at some point.

As Dr. Leroy Little Bear has told us, *if everything is animate, then everything has spirit and knowledge. If everything has spirit and knowledge, then all are like me. If all are like me, then all are my relations.*

Land acknowledgment is about the land, and the First Peoples of this land, and the relationship that was established.

Iika nai kso ko watsi yopa – we are all related. Which speaks to diversity, inclusion, and equality.

Elder Roy Bear Chief of the Siksika Nation
Espoom tah (Helper)
Mount Royal University alumnus (Social Work, 1994), and University of Calgary alumnus (Bachelor of Social Work, 1999; Master of Social Work, 2004)

YOU @ THE U

FIRST-YEAR GUIDANCE FROM A FRIENDLY STUDENT COUNSELLOR

What is this book about, and why do I need it?
How can a book help me get through my first year of university?

I'M A UNIVERSITY student counsellor with over twenty years of experience, and I know *everything* about how to live a happy life. I can take all of the stress out of your first year of university.

Actually...that's not completely true.

It's true that I have more than twenty years' experience as a university student counsellor, but my own life happiness and ability to manage stress are works-in-progress. In fact, it took me over forty years to take a real vacation, even longer to sort out my love life, and I'm still figuring out how to manage my stress, my time, and my clutter. I can't promise to take away all of life's stresses. No one can.

As for university, well, it's supposed to be challenging, but the transition into student life doesn't need to be completely overwhelming.

It was during that first real vacation that I experienced the spark of inspiration for this first-year student handbook. I called that initial draft "One Hundred and Five Ways to Manage Stress." It included five things I think every student should know about stress and a hundred possible interventions to help you get back into your zone: things such as drinking water, working out, and meditating...It was brilliant, accessible, and interesting.

Actually, according to the student volunteers who came to my focus group, "it was boring as @#%!" and felt "like a long lecture from Mom." Apparently, even the title sounded stressful.

Okay, so that was *not* the book I needed to write.

The students in that focus group already knew they needed to drink water and eat vegetables, but who has time for that during midterms? They told me that when classes were on, they were too stressed to read a book about stress. Maybe this was something they could pick up over the holiday break, but who needs a stress book then?

That student focus group changed my life and the focus of this book. The students said they didn't want to talk about "stress" per se, but they did share specific concerns about practical problems. How do you know if your university major is a good choice? How can you make friends in such a big place? How do you manage the massive workload and still get decent sleep? No one had prepared them for the transition to university. One student said, "It was like running into a wall, repeatedly," until they figured out how to get around it. Another said that "a heads-up on the academic life hacks we now know would have been nice." And they all said that stress just ends up being a way of life as you work your way through first year. They described it as a "silent weight that almost everyone carries" and "a pain you walk with every day."

Indeed, starting university is like breaking in a new pair of shoes: they're the nicest (and most expensive) pair you've ever owned, but right now they're rubbing your heels raw. You run around pretending your feet are fine, you make yourself too busy to notice, or you hesitate to talk about the pain because everyone else seems to be okay. Even though stress is the number one thing that brings students into counselling, I know that most students don't talk about their stress at all. The blisters are real though, and adjustment takes time.

I have waited years for someone else to write a book that helps new university students to adjust and succeed. I found sweet little stress books with puppies and rainbows on their covers, textbooks with lengthy chapters, and books that focus on supporting parents as they guide their children out the door and off to college. There's *Stress Management for Dummies,*[1] spiritual books on wellness, mindfulness apps, guides for managing roommate conflict, and books on how to position yourself for a great career. There are books full of quick tips and hacks that teach you how to *win* at university, but where was the book for overwhelmed or frightened new students who gather in our student counselling waiting room towards the end of September, shoulders slumped from the weight of worry (and from their enormous backpacks)?

Even better would be a book to give out before classes get underway to normalize the transition ahead and ease the burdens before they build up. This is my goal.

I've taken what I've learned from my career as a student counsellor and turned it into a handbook to support *your* first-year experience. I'm also posting materials and podcasts on my website (drjanetmiller.com) for you to use or pass along. In the pages ahead, I'll share highlights of what I've learned from thousands of university students who walked this path ahead of you. Their experience will guide you, because even though shoe styles change, the breaking-in process remains remarkably consistent.

The chapters of this book focus on a typical experience through the first term of university, but your story will of course vary from that path.

Think of it like this:

The first year of university is kind of like that new detective drama series everyone is watching. Even before the first episode is done, you have an idea of what's going to happen. There's going to be a crime that needs to be solved. There will be a twist and a missed clue. There will be a conflict between the detective and the sidekick, a flawed (but loveable) character, and an unlikeable suspect who we hope will be caught. Someone will have a standoff with the boss, and when there's a crisis about work-life balance, we aren't surprised. These plot elements show up in nearly every series, but you don't know the details or in what order they'll appear. The context and the characters vary, and that's what makes it interesting.

Your university experience will also be like that. Predictable in general, but not quite the same as anyone else's. You may find the guidance about managing the October Crash helpful now (Chapter 6), or you may want to read the section on choosing a major first (Chapter 9).

Look at the Table of Contents and flip through the chapters to get a sense of their key messages. Use the index to locate common topics as you need them.

As you read on, you'll find student experiences included in a number of ways. I've been gifted with stories, advice, and wisdom from many individuals, and when I present these to you, you'll see their first and last names noted along with their university connections. There are also composite stories based on students I've met over the years, and in these cases, only a first name is given. The elements of these composite scenarios are all real, but are not intended to resemble actual individuals.

I hope that every student will feel acknowledged somewhere in the words that follow, inclusive of age, family background, nationality, race, gender identity, sexual orientation, and responsibilities outside of university. My experiences as a white, cisgendered woman of settler descent have shaped my perspectives on the world, as have other aspects of my identity that are less obvious, including experiences with poverty, domestic violence, illness, and loss. Who you are, how you feel, and what you've been through will influence what stands out for you throughout this book, just as those parts of ourselves influence how we experience that trending detective drama.

As has been the case for me, there are times when your experience will make you stronger and more resilient; other times, you'll benefit from guidance and support. Each of our Canadian universities is equipped with a broad range of student services designed to provide that help, and I'm confident that when you have a need, you'll find support right on campus. At the end of this book, you'll find a list of typical student services, and I encourage you to search your campus website for more details.

So, how do you make a smooth transition into university without losing your mind? How do you pick a major when you don't know what's out there?

This book includes proven hacks for breaking in those new university shoes and will help you resolve some of those big questions.

It's not a guide about what you should do but rather what you should know to find your stride as you move towards mastery, confidence, and satisfaction in your student life.

To support the creation of this work, when I was invited into an undergraduate studies class (UGST 1101) taught by Glen Ryland at Mount Royal University, I asked that class of first-year students to reflect on their transition into university. I asked them this question: Knowing what you know now, what advice would you give to first-year students?

Their responses?

- Keep your head up. Don't get discouraged.
- Time management is very important in order to succeed in the semester.
- Don't be afraid to communicate with someone when you're struggling. There are plenty of people to help.
- Don't let assignments slide to make time for other assignments.
- Student learning services can help. Workshops are eye-opening.
- Keeping a calendar and getting ready for the day helps you get motivated for your classes.
- Reaching out to support systems is extremely important!
- It's okay to need help sometimes.
- Social connections are hard to make, but not impossible. Introduce yourself, and make sure you have people to turn to.
- Make your mental health and well-being a priority.
- You're more capable than you think.

Building on their advice, I'm confident that you'll walk away from this book feeling more at ease with how to

- organize yourself for successful course registration
- make the most out of student orientation

- connect with new people and build friendships
- work through imposter syndrome and wondering if you belong in university (spoiler alert: you do)
- reduce fear and embrace career uncertainty
- recover from setbacks, failures, and wrong turns
- steer through the sharp corners of academic life
- determine when an all-nighter is the right thing to do
- prepare for final exams.

Your first-year story will be one of a kind: completely unique, complicated, and captivating. It will have interesting twists, and you'll encounter unexpected characters along the way. Grounded in real stories, this book offers clues on how to navigate your first year, setting you up for a stellar second season. Feel that support in my words, let the student experience on these pages sink in.

It's time to begin this amazing journey into university life.

WHAT TO KNOW
BEFORE YOU GO

How do I find my student number? What's a prerequisite?
How do I register for classes and create a great timetable?
And what if I change my mind once the term starts?

TOWARDS THE END of high school, Kelly felt a mix of stress, exhaustion, and hope. The past few years hadn't been easy, and she was looking forward to getting out and moving on. The thick acceptance package embossed with the university logo stood out among the thin rejection letters, bringing with it the promise of more freedom and much-needed relief. For Kelly, the rest of high school suddenly felt doable.

Maybe you had a similar feeling of hope and excitement, even if your acceptance arrived in an email. Those final exams still matter, but with a university acceptance in hand, most of the pressure is off.

The academic experience that leads to university varies from coast to coast, and some people take a gap year (or a few) before heading into postsecondary. Regardless of where you are in this vast country – finishing a Pathways program in BC, attending CEGEP in Quebec, or completing Grade 12 in Alberta, Nunavut, or New Brunswick – you're likely focused on friendships, work experience, and good grades. Like Kelly, perhaps you're aiming to finish high school on a high note, or maybe you want to escape it as soon as humanly possible. Your summer will include some combination of resting, working, and hanging out.

As September draws closer, nervous excitement will settle in. Starting university is daunting, but once you're through the initial awkwardness, it's going to be great. Everyone will tell you it's a chance for a new beginning, more independence, and the opportunity to study what you're really interested in. The best years of your life are ahead.

SECONDARIES FROM COAST TO COAST

There's a lot of diversity among Canada's high schools. In most provinces and territories, high school runs from Grades 9 to 12. Exceptions include Alberta, where students are considered to be in high school from Grades 10 to 12, and Quebec, where high school runs from Grades 7 to 11. Some Canadian students graduate with a Dogwood Diploma, a Secondary V, or an OSSD.

To further confuse things, Grade 12 (if you had one) may have included Advanced Placement (AP) or International Baccalaureate (IB) classes. Your experiences may have included a work placement, an apprenticeship, or volunteer hours.

If you live in Quebec, you're likely part of the CEGEP (Collège d'enseignement général et professionnel) system. Most Québécois students attend a year or two of CEGEP before heading into post-secondary studies, and some may be much younger than their first-year peers when they arrive on campus.

This journey will begin with a welcome-to-campus experience. New-Student Orientation. First-Year Success. Frosh Week. Whatever they call it, it's an opportunity for the university to welcome new students into the fold. It's also the first opportunity to meet other new students. The flavour of your orientation will be unique, but the intention is the same across the board. Your university wants to welcome you into its community. You'll likely have a campus tour, a chance to hear from a few professors, and a meet-and-greet with other students from your program. They want you to find your classes, have some fun, and take on some school spirit. You'll have many events to choose from, but before you arrive, there are a few things you'll need to get organized.

Kelly's advice is to equip yourself with some basic resources before you head off to university.

Can you guess what's most important? Is it the hoodie or the bathrobe? A new binder or a laptop?

Nope. The first thing you need is a class schedule. It's not sexy, but it's the most important part of your university life.

The Registration Challenge

The FungBros YouTube team says that university registration basically equals your life.[1] If this is an overstatement, it's not by much. Your schedule influences your relationship with campus and is the backbone of first year. *Registration* means signing up for classes: when you register, you reserve your seat for the term, which determines your schedule. If you don't register, you'll show up for university with nothing to do. The only way to get into classes is to accept the registration challenge.

The challenge lies in the details. It's a complicated process full of technicalities and deadlines. There are required courses, and you may not have a choice on when to take them.

The good news? You can tailor your classes to fit your life. If you're an early riser and love to get things done before noon, then sign up for 8:00 a.m. classes. Want to avoid traffic jams or prefer to sleep in? Then set your schedule to begin after 10:00 a.m., or take night classes to keep your days free.

Most students find registration complicated, and it's okay to let a parent, friend, or supporter help. *But don't let them do it for you.* This is a skill you're going to need to master. You'll work through some frustration and disappointment, but in the end, you'll end up with a timetable you can live with and practical knowledge on how to work the system for the years ahead.

PRO TIP

Your university may have an online tool to help you build that ideal schedule. You might also find tools titled "Roadmap," "Achieve," or "Degree Navigator." Each is designed to show you the courses you'll need to complete your degree. Check your Registrar's webpage to see what's available.

If you have a chance to do an in-person, early-registration session, take it. These events are designed for new students, and they combine registration support with welcome events. If you go, you may have an opportunity to meet senior students, complete a campus tour, or register for courses months ahead of orientation.

To control chaos and help students get into the courses they need, registration usually opens in stages. Look through your acceptance package for details on *how* to register and *when* to register. It's like getting ready to buy tickets for an amazing concert: when tickets go on sale, you want to be ready. Seating is limited.

The Full-Time Advantage

I know this won't fit for all students, but as much as you can, enrol in full-time studies. Students who attend classes full-time have an advantage over their part-time peers. The data is clear. According to the *Even One Semester* report, full-time students "have consistently higher levels of engagement than always-part-time students."[2] Affectionately called full-time finishers, these students are about 15 percent more likely to complete first year and persist through to graduation. In a climate where more than a quarter of new students drop out before their second year of study, this is a significant edge that you'll want to have.

Yes, of course, there are also students who can succeed on a part-time basis. These part-time finishers might be students who work full-time while completing a degree part-time, or they may have switched between full- and part-time studies based on family needs, financial options, or other interests. Even one semester as a full-time student can give you an advantage, and the more experience you have as a full-time student, the stronger that advantage will become. You can achieve success in either situation, but if possible, please give yourself that full-time edge.

Getting Ready to Register

Your acceptance letter contains information about your program, the registration process, and your student ID number. It may also provide contact information for the university's Academic Advising office and likely explains how to find the university's course calendar online. You'll need to know the title and number (e.g., English 1101) of each course you want to take, and you'll need a section number too (there might be twelve sections of English 1101, each offered at a different time of day or day of the week).

ACADEMIC ADVISORS

Universities offer advising as a free service. You can rely on your academic advisor for accurate information about university policies, procedures, resources, and programs. Advisors will help you select courses and chart out a path to graduation. They'll know which courses you need to take for your degree, and they'll help you understand majors, minors, combined degrees, transfer programs, and so on. They'll also meet with you to evaluate your progress and revise your goals as needed. Some universities have a general advising office, while others have advisors embedded in faculties, schools, or programs. Go to your university's website and search for academic advising for more information.

Required Courses and Electives or Options

Your acceptance letter might list the courses required for your degree, or it might outline options for a more general first year of studies. Remember that you can contact your academic advisor for information if you're in doubt about what you're required to take. Many first-year students wait until there's a problem before reaching out to their academic advisor. Know that it's okay, and in fact encouraged, to see them, even if it's only to check in or have them review your course selection.

Most degrees also include electives or option courses – and here's where you get quite a bit of flexibility about what you can add into your degree. You might consider taking a class you're interested in but don't want to major in – or perhaps you want to take something that seems altogether new. Don't get too discouraged if you end up taking something off the wall – that unexpected class might be surprisingly good.

STUDENT STORY

Looking back, I wish I had just taken my mandatory courses during first year and held off on making decisions about those optional courses. In my university, the GNED (General Education) 1101 course changes focus every year or two based on who's teaching it, but I didn't know that. I assumed that GNED 1101 was just a regular standard course, and so I signed up for it first term. My section focused on the Republic of Plato, not my preference but, whatever, I needed the course, so I did it. In my second year, a new prof came on and started teaching a section of GNED 1101. This one focused on the Oka Crisis and the Mohawk resistance at Kanesatà:ke. I would have loved that course, but I couldn't enrol because I already had that course credit. I wish I had waited, but I didn't know. I'd recommend talking to your academic advisor to get clear information on how options work at your university. – ANDREA HERON, Psychology, Mount Royal University Alumna

Lectures, Tutorials, and Labs

Each of your classes will include a lecture. To make scheduling more complicated, sometimes you'll also see tutorials or labs associated with a single course, and there might be variations in how these courses are offered. For example, a three-hour lecture might run as

- three one-hour blocks each week
- two ninety-minute blocks
- one three-hour block.

That same class may have three hours of lecture combined with two hours of lab time or a weekly tutorial, or both.

Read the fine print. If you've got doubts, ask an academic advisor.

What are these components like? Lectures are set up like high-school classes. They're instructional talks given by a professor, and they contain the bulk of the content for the course. Labs are hands-on experiential learning opportunities, often involving group work, experiments, or simulations. Tutorials bring students together in small groups to discuss specific ideas or readings. They're led by the professor or a graduate teaching assistant (TA).

Deciphering the Details

Through the registration process you're going to run into a lot of strange terms and a load of university acronyms. Here are some common ones you might see on your registration site or class schedule.

Semester and Year Notations: F23, W24

Most universities will have a Fall, Winter, Spring, and maybe Summer semester. Typically, the Fall term runs from September to December, Winter runs from January to April, and Spring runs through May and June. Summer courses scheduled in July or August may also be available. Terms are often paired with the year – for example, F23 means Fall term 2023, and W24 means Winter 2024. When you're signing up for classes, you'll likely need to select the term you're registering for.

Weekday and Time Slot Notations: R 1500–1620

Academic schedules often use a letter to symbolize the weekday and may list course times on a twenty-four-hour clock. There is no universal format for this. UBC starts and ends classes on the hour or half hour (9:30–11:00, 13:00–14:30) while Mount Royal University starts on the hour or half hour but gives ten minutes between classes (11:00 a.m.–12:20 p.m., 2:30 p.m.–3:50 p.m.). Dalhousie University also structures breaks between classes, and their system uses the twenty-four-hour clock (1305–1425, 1035–1125). Every university is a bit different.

Weekdays might be listed by a single letter, typically M, T, W, and F (straightforward), but R? That's used for *Thursday*. I'm not sure who came up with that convention, but I bet that it has confused thousands of new students. And R 1500–1620? *That* means the course runs on Thursdays, from 3:00 p.m. to 4:20 p.m.

CRN

The course registration number (CRN) is likely something you'll only need to know when you register for the course. You can think of it as a catalogue number used to identify a particular course, at a particular time, in a particular year. At my university, CRNs are five digits long. Math 1101 in the Fall of 2022 might have a CRN of 23456, but in the Fall of 2023 that same course might have a CRN of 34567. Each course registration number is a unique identifier, and you'll need to have yours ready when you go online to register for your classes.

Block Courses

These are like regular courses but condensed into a brief time frame. Instead of spreading the class across a Fall or Winter semester, the university offers a block course that packs a whole semester's worth of material into just a week or two. These classes often run five days a week before the regular semester begins. You're unlikely to have block courses in your first year, but you might see them as an option for year two.

Customizing Your Schedule

Your challenge is to schedule your required classes and chosen electives into a customized timetable that suits your style. Two people can take the same classes but have entirely different schedules.

Start by making a list of the courses you want to take this year (required courses and your preferred options), then check the course calendar to see how many times each class is offered. Most courses will be offered several times each term. However, if something is only offered once and you need that course, then you're stuck with that timing. Plug that course into your schedule first and then build the rest of your timetable around it.

Next, look at your optional courses and fit those around your priorities. It's a problem with many solutions, which can quickly get overwhelming, but it also means that there's more than one way to win.

In this example, Kelly and Mario both register for full-time studies and have the same set of five classes. Each class involves a three-hour lecture, and a few also have a tutorial or lab.

Courseload for Kelly and Mario
English 101: three hours of lecture, one-hour tutorial
Math 101: three hours of lecture, two hours of labs
Chemistry 101: three hours of lecture, two hours of labs
Astronomy 101: three hours of lecture
Sociology 101: three hours of lecture

Before registration opens, Mario and Kelly each plot out their preferred plan. Kelly wants Fridays off for work and ski trips, while Mario wants to avoid early classes to sleep in most days.

The chemistry class lecture is only offered once this term, on Mondays, and since it is a required course, both Kelly and Mario add it to their schedule. The chemistry lab is offered several times per week, so they have some flexibility.

For Math 101, they have choices, but the labs are tied to the lectures. Kelly wants the three-hour lecture on Tuesday afternoons, but that would mean a Friday lab. Looking at her options, she finds another section that has two ninety-minute lectures instead of a three-hour one. They start early, but 8:00 a.m. works fine in Kelly's life, so she takes that option. Mario decides to take English across three days (a one-hour class three times a week instead of a three-hour block once a week) because this means his mornings will be completely open for sleeping or working out.

The schedules they come up with suit their preferences, and when registration opens, this is what they'll aim to get.

When it comes time to register, Kelly and Mario know it will be a race to secure their preferred classes. To reduce stress, they each create a secondary schedule to fall back on in case their first-choice classes are full. When the registration gates open, they will be ready.

What Are Your Friends Doing?

When choosing courses, especially your electives, try to break out of the high-school mentality of sticking with your friends or sticking with what you know. You'll make new friends when you branch out, and students often say that being in a class of strangers allows

Kelly's preferred schedule (long weekends)

	MON.	TUES.	WED.	THURS.	FRI.
8:00 A.M.	English	Math		Math	
9:00 A.M.			English tutorial		
10:00 A.M.		Math lab		Math lab	
11:00 A.M.					
12:00 P.M.		Chemistry lab	Chemistry lab		
1:00 P.M.	Chemistry			Astronomy	
2:00 P.M.			Sociology		
3:00 P.M.					
4:00 P.M.					
5:00 P.M.					

Mario's preferred schedule (a late start)

	MON.	TUES.	WED.	THURS.	FRI.
8:00 A.M.					
9:00 A.M.					
10:00 A.M.					
11:00 A.M.	English		English		English
12:00 P.M.					English tutorial
1:00 P.M.	Chemistry	Chemistry lab	Chemistry lab	Astronomy	
2:00 P.M.		Math	Sociology		Math lab
3:00 P.M.					
4:00 P.M.					
5:00 P.M.					

them to connect with a new crowd. Maybe you'll meet your new best friend, a new crush, or your new nemesis... all three can shape your life in a positive direction.

Kelly's Tips

HAVING JUST GONE THROUGH THE REGISTRATION PROCESS, HERE'S WHAT I RECOMMEND:

Actually read through your acceptance package. Mine had a pamphlet explaining how and when to register. Check yours for directions and deadlines.

Course registration is a lot like buying concert tickets. When the system opens, you want to be ready, or you won't get the seats you want (or, worse yet, the class will be sold out).

I emailed the academic advising office at the university, and they were amazing. I couldn't do an in-person appointment (I lived too far away), but we did talk over the phone. They explained what courses were required for my program, showed me how to access the University Calendar of courses on the website, and walked me through what *optional courses or electives* meant. Totally worth it.

My older brother told me to build a few possible schedules. Start with the courses you NEED and the timeslots you WANT, then create a Plan B and a Plan C in case those courses are already full when you go to register for them.

It's likely you won't get your first choices for every class, so prepare to be flexible, and get ready for some frustration. I had one class that was only offered once in the Fall term, so I rushed to get that one first and then scheduled my other classes around it.

If the schedule you get sort of sucks, don't give up. You'll have a chance to move courses around at the beginning of the term. My university calls it "drop and add." It's like having a free trial for a class. If you're registered, and you like it, stay in it... but if it seems awful (boring prof, too far across campus, terrible timing, whatever), then you can drop out with no consequence. When someone drops a class that was full, that spot becomes available. During those days, you can jump on those open seats and add the class to your schedule. Some courses keep a waitlist, but at my university, I had to just keep checking back to see if a spot was available. Annoying... but in my case it paid off.

But Wait... What Does Restricted Access Mean?

Sometimes you'll be interested in a course that is reserved for students in a specialized program. You won't be able to register unless you get special permission. Universities often call these classes "restricted," "reserved," or "closed." For example, the class Writing for Television 1000 might be open only to communication students, or the 10:00 a.m. physics time slot might be reserved for science majors only. This helps ensure that students who need those classes to graduate have access to those spots. Once students who need those classes have registered, other students may be allowed in. This *special* permission may be granted by the chair of the academic department, but usually there needs to be a compelling reason to allow you in.

What's a Prereq?

You're likely to come across prerequisites in the registration process. Sometimes a course will have conditions that you need to satisfy before you can enrol in it. For example, Philosophy 2201 might require that you take Philosophy 1101 first. In that case, Philosophy 1101 is considered a prerequisite for Philosophy 2201. Prereqs are listed in your course calendar, and the online system will usually block you from registering for a class you can't yet take. If you want to challenge that decision, make your request before registration opens. Maybe you have an equivalent course from another institution, an advanced high-school class that meets the prereq requirement, or some kind of relevant work experience that helped you develop your expertise in this area. You can ask the department chair to waive the prerequisite requirement based on that justification. At other times, you may be allowed to take the prereq at the same time as the next-level course (e.g., both Calculus 101 and Calculus 202 in the same semester) – but, as you can imagine, taking that first level first will help you succeed in the next.

Most first-year classes don't have a prerequisite, but your second-year classes might.

Alternative Delivery Models
Sometimes universities will offer their classes in multiple formats – online, in person, or through blended delivery. *Online* means that you don't need to physically come to campus to take the course; *in person* is completely on campus; and *blended delivery* involves some combination of the two. Pick the format that fits best with your academic goals and lifestyle, but whenever you can (and especially in your first year), I recommend taking your courses in person on campus.

When Registration Goes Wrong
The great thing about registration is that you have some flexibility about what you take and when you take it. The awful thing about registration is that you won't necessarily get what you want. This happened to Mario. He really wanted that English class that ran at 11:00 a.m., but by the time he got online to register, that section was full. He got stuck with the 8:00 a.m. Monday class. While Kelly was thrilled to land a seat in that section, for Mario, it was depressing.

Be prepared to find out that the course you're interested in is already full; or worse, you might find it's not even offered this term.

If it's full, put your name on the waitlist. You can also email the professor to ask if the course cap (the maximum number of students allowed in the course) might increase. You can gauge your hope level based on that insider information and either hold out to see if you get in or move on to your Plan B. If it's not offered, then you're out of luck. In the years ahead, you can consider an online option from another university and then ask for a course transfer credit. But for your first year, I'd recommend sticking with your university's regular course offerings.

What If You Change Your Mind?
Universities typically have a few supports in place to help you if you find yourself in a course you don't want, don't like, or aren't succeeding in. Imagine you've followed all of Kelly's advice, but in the first few days of classes you realize you'd rather be in another section of

QUICK TIP ⚡

There's nothing worse than when you need a class as a prerequisite and you can't get into it because you procrastinated. Registration is a task you don't want to put off.

English (better time slot? better teacher? your new best friend is in it?). Or what happens if a few weeks in you just want to dump the course altogether (lost interest? best friend has turned on you? failing grade?). Most universities have a drop/add period during which you can change your schedule without paying a penalty. It's a small window of time – usually just two or three days – when the university provides students with a last chance to shop around for other courses. You won't be charged for classes you drop, and your transcript won't show the changes you make. (This is not the same as *withdrawing* from a class. Withdrawing is something you can do after the drop-and-add period is over, up until the withdrawal deadline. When you withdraw from a course you don't get your tuition back. While the withdrawal will be listed on your transcript, your GPA won't be impacted. Given that a "W" on your transcript could have other ramifications, choose it sparingly. If you want more information on this situation, talk with your academic advisor and flip ahead to Chapter 13.)

Consider Mario's situation. He's arrived on campus and has started classes, but the reality of that 8:00 a.m. Monday class hits him hard. He pushes himself to be there, but he hates every minute of it. It's not the teacher, the commute, or the syllabus; it's the timing. Mario and mornings don't get along. Luckily for Mario (and all students), the drop/add period exists.

The drop/add period is chaotic, though, and to get what you want you sometimes need to be on your toes. Some universities will let you join a waitlist. As students drop out of a class, their spot opens up for people on the waitlist. Other institutions might send an alert when a "watched" class opens up; whoever responds to that message first wins the spot.

Unfortunately, Mario's university doesn't have a watch-list or an alert system. There's nothing automatic about it. To get his coveted

11:00 a.m. class, he kept an eye on the registration system, watching for an open spot. He wasn't sure what he'd do if it didn't work out, but, luckily, he didn't have to face that decision. A spot opened up late on the second night, and he pounced on it. Once the new seat was secured, he dropped his 8:00 a.m. class with glee.

STUDENT TIP ⚑
I felt lucky to get the course I wanted through drop and add ... but by the time I was officially enrolled, I had missed two full weeks of the class. My advice? Register early. And do everything you can to get the classes you want. Only use drop and add if you're desperate. – MARIO

Key Messages

☆ Getting your course schedule organized is PRIORITY ONE.

☆ Course selection is a skill worth mastering. Ask for help, but don't let anyone else register for you.

☆ Work out your ideal course schedule on paper first (before you head to the online registration portal).

☆ Get your required courses into your schedule first, then plot your options around them.

☆ Have a Plan B *and* a Plan C ready to go in case courses are full. Making two back-up course schedules will take time, but if you run into roadblocks when you try to register, you'll be glad to have these alternatives ready.

☆ Register as soon as you can; it's not something you want to procrastinate on.

☆ Drop-and-add gives you a second chance to switch your classes around, but it's a chaotic process, and if you do get in, you'll have to rush to catch up on what you've missed. Do your best to get the courses you want now.

☆ If in doubt, talk with your academic advisor. Don't know who this is? Then search for *advising* on your university's webpage and email or call the main office.

MOVING
(EVEN IF YOU'RE NOT)

Will I miss out on all the good things if I'm living at home this year?
As an international student, is there an advisor I can connect with?
I'm moving into student housing on campus, what should I bring?

BECOMING A UNIVERSITY student is going to change dozens of things about your life, including your daily schedule, your relationships, and your living environment. Here, we're going to focus on two kinds of movements common to first-year life: moving up and moving out.

As soon as you accept the offer of postsecondary studies, it's going to feel like you're moving up in the world. You are moving up in your level of education from CEGEP or high school, or perhaps you're coming back into school from a gap-year adventure or from a job you've outgrown. Many of you will also be living at home while you go through these changes. Living at home can pose opportunities and challenges, which are well worth reflecting on here. The "Moving Out" section acknowledges that some students move across the world to study at a university while others might only move down the road. Some students will be on their own for the first time while some will be moving into student residence. Whatever your life situation, change will happen as you enter into your first year.

Moving Up but Staying Home

There may be significant upsides to staying at home, including emotional support, no rent, and easy access to meals or laundry. There might be comfort in the familiarity of home, even if it's not a terrific situation. When you stay in the space you know, you have fewer things to adjust to. Fewer changes ahead. For some students, moving out isn't a viable financial option, and for many, the benefits of staying home outweigh the other options.

If you're staying at home while going to university, many of the things that have become routine will need to shift. The family dynamic will be altered, patterns and schedules will change, and you'll have to cope with commuting. Students who live at home have certain advantages, but they also have to make adjustments, and they must make a conscious effort to connect with campus. They may find it harder than students who don't live at home to break away from comfortable habits or make space for new friendships. Here are some tips to help manage those changes.

Talk about the New Normal

Living at home can present challenges around privacy, self-reliance, and autonomy. There will also be changes in work patterns, friendship time, and extracurricular activities. Many after-school activities that were common in high school will drop off as students become busier and their priorities shift.

Talk with your parents, friends, and supporters about their expectations for you (and your expectations for them) as you transition into university. Explain what is important to you when it comes to boundaries, leisure time, curfews, finances, chores, and access to resources – and find out what is important to them.

While university may increase your autonomy and freedom in some ways, you'll likely find you have reduced free time and less energy. You may need to shift your responsibilities in your personal life. For example, Martha, who lives with her partner and their two kids, felt okay forgoing the children's bath time but didn't want to miss out on their bedtime routine. Jiang wanted to keep up with family meals on weekends but likely wouldn't be home for dinner through the week.

Take the guesswork out of the situation and talk with your family about what you want (and need) first year to look like. For Kailin, the situation was a bit more complicated, and to say that her home wasn't conducive to studying would have been an understatement.

She couldn't afford to move out, but she also knew that she wouldn't find the quiet she needed to study at home. Her "big talk" was with her employer, who let her use the back office for school work when she wasn't on shift. Kailin relied on that space through the first eight weeks or so and then slowly transitioned to studying in the university library.

Upgrade Your Space

University students need room to spread out and study and more space to store their textbooks. Privacy is important when you need to focus, and students say that moving to postsecondary changes their style and decor. Consider ways to refresh your surroundings.

- Phillip moved his study space out of his bedroom and set up a spot by the dining room. He hoped this would help give some separation between his school work and his downtime.

- Jiang cleared out some of their old memorabilia to make room for textbooks. They also moved their desk to the window for better light.

- Since a distraction-free study space was at the top of Martha's list, the family cleared out the basement storage area and created a space where she could work behind a closed door.

- Kailin felt that being at home wasn't going to be conducive to studying at all. She found a satchel at a thrift store that could hold her laptop, headphones, binder, and study supplies so she could study elsewhere.

Make the Most of Your Commute

The majority of first-year students commute, so take comfort – you're not alone. If you're going to commute, you might as well enjoy it. First-year arts student Jiang has a long drive every day. To make it more enjoyable, they've mastered the travel kit, which includes snack foods that are easy to eat on the road, a full bottle of water, iced coffee, downloaded podcasts and audiobooks, and one of those

COMMUTER STUDENT SERVICES

York University publishes recommended playlists for its commuter students, and Ryerson started a commuter student hostel for nights when staying on campus makes sense. The University of Guelph employs a coordinator to support the commuter experience and has a peer-helper program specifically for students who live off campus. King's University hosts special events just for commuter students, and McMaster hosts an Off-Campus Students' Society. If you look at your university's website for commuter student resources, you'll likely find programming and supports tailored to fit your needs.

plug-in heating pads for the colder mornings. Because their car is far from fancy, they have a roadside service membership and an Uber account to use in emergencies. On the advice of a friend, Jiang posted a carpooling want-ad on their community centre's social page, and by the end of September found another student to share the drive with. Their schedules align three days a week, and commuting together has helped lessen the costs of gas and parking. Jiang loves the company and really looks forward to this social time on the road.

Kailin approaches her commute to school as an opportunity for silence. She loves being unreachable, whether she's cycling or driving, and she's found that the ride in is good for her mental health. It's become a bit of a sanctuary, offering time to relax and unwind. Kailin lives close enough to the university to bike to school on the days the weather is good and when her bag is light. So far, that's three out of five days a week. She did not go for a parking pass, but instead opted to rent one of those high-end bike lockers. She was told that bike thefts are common, and the locker gives her good peace of mind.

At first, Phillip, a first-year science student, didn't like his eighty-minute transit trip to campus, but he now admits that it's grown into a productive and enjoyable experience. He uses his laptop on the forty-minute train ride to draft out papers or complete assignments and then reviews his class notes or studies from cue

STUDENT TIP ♟
For the drivers out there – look around for free street parking first. The walk in to campus will be worth the cash you save. If you have to park on campus, then balance out your fees by saying no to a locker. Just use your trunk instead. Keep your gym gear and a change of shoes in there. I store my 50lb Chem text in my car along with Advil, tampons, deodorant, a hairbrush, and a pillow. You might think that napping in your car is strange, but midterms might change your mind. I also stash some emergency cash, in case I need to transit or cab it home. – MYCA

cards while on the bus. What started as a long and boring commute has been transformed into short and focused study sessions. As a bonus, Phillip finds that much of his evening time has been freed up.

In all three of these cases, there was no getting around the commute. If you have to do it, you might as well enjoy it. Either make your commute productive or embrace the opportunity to be off-duty.

Build a Sense of Community
Regardless of your reason for staying home, you'll need to be mindful of some serious drawbacks. They extend beyond commuting and pertain to the social and emotional parts of university life. Students who stay at home while they attend university – especially those who also have a close circle of friends from CEGEP or high school, and those who have jobs with significant hours – often hold back on making new connections in university. They either don't have the time for new friendships, or they don't really need them.

Not making new friends is a problem because university social connections are important. Friendships forged at university often withstand the test of time, but they also offer practical advantages, such as broadening our understanding of people and cultures, opening us up to new perspectives, and increasing our networks. School connections also make course work easier. For example, you may meet a second-year student who just took the class you've enrolled in, or a peer could point you in the direction of a great community resource. Other students will also tell you about funding deadlines or might show you where the events with free food are taking place. Being connected to the social fabric of the university will give you many opportunities for fun. When you live at home, you need to be intentional about spending social time on campus.

Make a point of being on campus even if you don't have a class. If you treat university like high school – for instance, leaving as soon as classes are over – then you're going to miss out on social activities. Spend time on campus walking around and exploring the spaces. Arrive early to your classes so you can meet people in the hallways. If you stay after class, you're bound to start making connections. Give the following a go:

- If possible, get a locker so you can dump your stuff.
- Go to the cafeteria and check out the library.
- Use campus services.
- Look at people as you walk in the halls. Familiar faces will begin to stand out.
- Look for places to lounge. Every university has spaces with comfortable seating and places to charge your phone or plug in your laptop, heat up your food, or have a nap. Locate your options and start getting comfortable.
- Join a club or go to a student hub or community space and stick around for evening events. The life of the university is there for you to discover.

Moving Out

Many of you might need to relocate to take the program you want or have the experience you crave. Whether you move to Canada to be an international student or move across town to live in residence or in off-campus housing, there are services that will help you make the most of your move.

QUICK TIP ⚡
When you live off campus, you miss out on a lot of social connections. To start building your group, ask new classmates to meet up for a beer or coffee. Set up a few individual meetings, but then overlap them so your new friends get the chance to meet one another. As your new friends start to connect, your peer group will grow.

STUDENT TIP 🪧

If you plan to use a U-Haul –
seriously, book it as soon as you
send in your acceptance letter. I
swear they must do most of their
yearly business between August
31st and September 2nd. – MILLEY

International Moves

According to the Government of Canada's *Building on Success: International Educational Strategy, 2019–2024*, the number of international students choosing to study in Canada is at an all-time high.[1] In 2018 alone, Canadian schools hosted 721,205 international students, most studying at the post-secondary level. Around the world, student mobility is growing. Mary Dwyer reported in *Maclean's* magazine that institutions such as UBC, McGill, Bishop's University, and the University of Toronto now welcome more than a quarter of their first-year undergraduate cohort as international students.[2]

I'm delighted that your educational pathway not only led you to Canada but also to this book. In addition to regular student services, you'll have opportunities to connect with international student services. Your acceptance package will outline contact information for your university's international student's office, and people there will be able to answer your questions about culture, language, study permits, temporary resident permits, health insurance, and travel support. If they can't answer your questions, then they'll refer you to someone who can. Best of all, international student service offices will help you connect with other students, including local students and other international students.

Learning about Canadian culture – and adjusting to Canadian winters – will take time, but it's worth the effort. Connecting with a community of other students and spending time in the Canadian outdoors will be two highlights of your undergraduate experience.

STUDENT STORY

University education is a huge investment in your future self, especially as an international student. What it takes to earn excellent grades can be more demanding than what it would be in your original country. If English isn't your first language, you may find it even more challenging to adjust to the Canadian life, as well as your university life. But don't stress out too much about it! I am in the same boat with you.

The biggest piece of advice I have for other international students is really to seek how they would want to get involved. Going to classes and coming back to your dorm may not be a problem at first, but once you get used to your life in Canada, you may feel a bit lost or uncertain without more connections. Although you come to Canada to get an education, it alone won't fulfill your experience here, in my opinion.

What helps me are the plentiful resources available on campus, such as Student Learning Services and the Peer Mentorship Program at my university [and] also countless non-academic programs, such as Stepping Up and Language Partners Program. Start seeking what and how you would like to get involved at your university. Support is there and ready to accelerate your future.

– MIZUKI OSHITA, undergraduate student, Mount Royal University, from Kobe, Japan

Moving into Student Housing

If you're moving away from home and into residence, you'll be moving into a community experience. Student housing includes individual rooms in apartments or townhomes, shared accommodations in traditional dorm houses, and houses designed to accommodate you and your family.

There are a few essentials you'll want on hand. Be that new student who has the great bathrobe, fuzzy slippers, or study blanket. You'll be surprised how often you use these items outside of your room. To make the place comfy and more like home, consider purchasing a foam mattress and bring a comfortable pillow and bedding, a room deodorizer, sticky tack or removable adhesive wall hangers, and lights that give the vibe you want.

STUDENT TIP 📌

Buy a new mattress if you can swing it. The ones in residence are often thin and strangely slippery, and used ones are a bit gross. Topping up is also good – I saw foam-mattress toppers on sale at the bookstore. – PAUL

STUDENT TIP 📌

Don't do your laundry on Sundays! The lineups will be awful, and someone will dump your stuff out if you're not there the minute your cycle ends. Waiting around for a dryer is NOT the way to spend a weekend. Avoid the traffic jam and get it done on a weekday. – MARC

If you share a bathroom or use the shower at the gym, get yourself a pair of flip-flops...You can imagine why. A few good towels, a portable shower tote, a big wall calendar, and extra shelving are also very useful. (Back in my day, makeshift shelves were made of reclaimed plastic milk crates, under a plank of wood – today's equivalent might involve Kijiji or a trip to IKEA). Laundry soap pods and a large, easy-to-carry laundry bag will certainly improve your life.

If you have a kitchen in your residence room, then you might need a kettle, a great cooking pot, and some basic dishes and cutlery. If you have a standard residence room sofa, it could likely use a few cushions to make it more comfortable, and an area rug might make the place feel a bit more like home.

Your university residence might have a move-in packing list, and you can certainly find countless other move-in suggestions online.

Should you need them, fully accessible housing units are available (to accommodate a wheelchair, for example). You might also be able to request a specialized learning community (like a first-year learning commons or an engineering floor). In either case, hold off on buying furniture until you've seen the space and have tried moving things around to suit your needs.

When it comes time to pack up and go off to university, pack like you're prepping for a long trip. You want to bring enough to be comfortable but not so much that you're bogged down.

QUICK TIP ⚡

Regardless of where you decide to live, here are a few things that students tell me are essentials:

- BACKPACK: A book bag is the mainstay of every student's life – something that's got a bit of style, is comfortable over your shoulder, and the right size. It should be large enough to carry your binder or laptop but small enough to carry around all day.

- LAPTOP: If you can get one, a laptop or large tablet with a keyboard will make your life much easier. You'll have flexibility when it comes to where to study and with whom, and you can use it in most classes to take notes (although actually writing things down on paper is best for your memory). If you can't purchase one, check with your campus library to see if they loan laptops out.

- PORTABLE CHARGER: Having a charger on hand will likely prevent a crisis at some point.

- EXTERNAL HARD DRIVE: Useful to transport files and also to back things up.

- GIFTS: Remind your supporters that giving you cash, cookies, and encouragement will help, as will gift cards for campus vendors and grocery stores within walking distance.

Note: Subscriptions for entertainment channels, delivery services, and food pickup are useful and in high demand, but I caution against putting these in place right away. If you're too comfortable in your space, you run the risk of binge-watching TV series instead of getting out and making friends. Once you find your school rhythm and develop solid study habits, these entertainment services can be amazing to have. Get them too early, though, and they encourage isolation and reinforce disengagement.

Off-Campus Housing

If you plan to move into off-campus housing, you'll need to need to secure your own place and furnish it. You'll likely need just about everything mentioned above (including my tips on making peace with your commute into campus; see p. 24).

Choosing the Place. Most universities have off-campus housing offices ready to support you in your search. Supports may also be available through your student union. The student housing board usually advertises apartments for rent and vacancies in shared houses, along with general community-based rental listings. Take your time as you browse online, and get support from your family, university, and friends. Make it your goal to see at least three places in person before making a decision. You may want to consider renting a room in a house shared by other students, or you may want to live on your own. Some vacancy boards make special mention of queer-friendly housing, and LGBTQ2SIA+ centres often help aid in that search.

Some students aim to rent rooms or suites in houses close to school; they live with families or single people who aren't students. Another alternative might be renting a place with people you already know – your partner, say, or your friends. Barbara needed an apartment that could accommodate her wheelchair and decided to focus her search on larger apartment buildings. If you have deal-breaker needs (such as your cat or a parking space with a plug-in), Barbara's advice is to call ahead.

Plan to begin your search two months in advance and aim to pick the place that suits your needs for safety, privacy, budget, and proximity. When you're thinking about total cost, remember to factor in parking fees or transit commute time, laundry access, and utility payments along with the monthly rent.

⌐ **STUDENT STORY** ⌐

My first place was a basement apartment close to campus. The windows were pretty big, and it had a bathtub. But best of all, I was allowed to bring my cat. I could walk to school easily, and with no transit or parking to pay, it fit within my budget just fine. – ELISE

Leasing Decisions. Some university towns seem to offer only one-year lease options for students. A twelve-month lease means that you're agreeing to pay rent for twelve months, whether you live there or not. This might be fine if you plan to stay for the summer, but many off-campus students want to go home for that four-month break. If you plan to spend summer back home, then ask about subletting, or look for an eight-month lease or a month-to-month rental agreement. Some places will also ask for a co-signer – someone with a strong credit rating who will promise to pay the rent if you can't. This isn't unheard of in the student market, but it's often not required. It's nice when utilities (water, heat) are included in your rent because managing your budget is easier when expenses are predictable. If you have to pay your own utilities, make sure to set up your accounts before you move in. You're going to want a hot shower and cell service on that first day. Utility costs can also vary a great deal from September to January. Be prepared to see larger bills in those colder months.

Landlord and tenant acts vary widely by province, so don't assume that you know the rules for your university's area. The off-campus student housing office will be a good source of information, or search online to find the governmental resource for your area.

STUDENT STORY

My best friend and I, we went for a two-bedroom apartment in a high-rise near downtown. It had a good view, and our parents liked that it had a security entrance. Heat was included, but we had to get used to paying our own internet bills. The train into campus was easy, and living together was awesome. No regrets. – MARGARET

Apartment Essentials. You're going to need some basic furniture, cookware, utensils, bedding, and towels. You can find a lot of apartment checklists online, and in addition to those key items, I recommend you stock up on supplies at the beginning of the year, if you can, especially if you won't have easy access to a car. Many students browse and scavenge garage sales, thrift stores, Kijiji, and their own basements as they prepare to move out on their own.

Sort Out Parking or Transit

If you're not living right on campus, map out the best routes to and from campus. Some schools have transit cards or passes, and some have free parking available in nearby communities. Some university parking lots are so massive that the school uses shuttle buses to take commuters from parking spots onto campus. Look for discounts on car-share programs and, of course, consider biking or walking if you can. There are many options to check out.

> **STUDENT TIP**
> Get your parking and your locker figured out first. I'm on a waitlist 'cause I didn't. It sucks. – ALYSSA

STUDENT STORY

Mizuki Oshita, an international student at Mount Royal University, has learned to dress in layers while taking transit. She shares this story:

"A word of warning for my fellow international students. Since I don't have a car, I have had to rely on public transportation. Last year, I went with my exchange-student friends to see a varsity hockey game. After the game ended, I had to walk and wait outside for the bus for nearly thirty minutes in the freezing cold weather. I really thought I was going to pass out from the cold, and I cried. It was the first time ever that I cried because of the weather. Another friend, who is also an international student, experienced a similar incident where it was too cold and she cried too. I am learning that in Canada, it feels much colder at night without the sun. If you'll be out for most of the day, bring a jacket."

Key Messages

☆ Whether commuting or moving (or both!), you're going to have to adjust to make the most of the experience.

☆ For commuters:

> Change up your room and your routines.

> Make the most of the commute by either embracing the downtime or seizing the chance to study.

> Sort out your parking plan early.

> You're going to have to make more efforts to stay on campus and build friendships. These will be worth the effort but building community takes time.

☆ For movers:

> Bring a few sentimental pieces from home with you.

> Bring basics for your kitchen and plan to master at least one great recipe.

> Laundry is daunting but doable.

> A comfy bed, a good towel, and flip-flops are essential.

> The social world will be there waiting for you – get out and embrace it. Get involved.

ORIENTATION AND WELCOME

Do I have to go to New Student Orientation?
Is frosh week still a thing? Is it scary?
I have a lot of orientation events to choose from,
which ones are most important to attend?

SEPTEMBER BRINGS LOTS of energy to campus. Nervous energy courses through the parking lots and down the halls. It's part adrenalin, part sweat, and part Axe cologne.

New students gather in silent clumps waiting for events to begin, enacting a kind of social distancing that hasn't been caused by a global pandemic. Senior student volunteers and university staff do their best to create connections in these early moments, but for the most part, students are quiet, alone, and awkward. Lots of fake phone work. Everyone is nervous.

What to Expect

Some universities will welcome you as part of a crowd of thousands, and others will host smaller events just for your program or cohort. All will work creatively to help you connect with campus. Traditional elements of orientation include pep rallies and keynote speeches, concerts, frosh activities, and exhibition-type sporting events. Some institutions will offer parts of their orientation online: the president's welcome might be posted as a video, or they might offer a virtual campus tour.

Even though some events may be streamed, if you can get to campus to be part of the community, please do. Universities thread numerous student events throughout the first weeks of classes. You'll experience outdoor events and small-group activities intended to facilitate student connections. Late-night movies in the park, organized campus tours, and grocery runs for residence students are common. Orientation and social meet-ups might be offered across multiple time slots to accommodate smaller crowds (for program introductions, carnival games, slam-dunk contests), there may be larger concerts, or travelling musicians might weave their way around campus. Parties will happen. Beer may be consumed.

STUDENT TIP ⚑
No need to overdress for NSO [New Student Orientation]. I wore a tie. Don't do that. – JAKE

You don't have to go to all events, but you should go to a few. In a survey of those who attended orientation at Mount Royal University, students raved about the campus tour, the chance to meet others from the same program, and having an opportunity to hear from professors before classes got underway. University leaders will talk about their hopes for your education, and you might hear a panel of alumni (graduates of your program) talk about their university experience. Most students say that orientation gave them a good feel for the place, which made starting classes less intimidating.

Orientation has different flavours at different universities, but all orientation programs will be student-focused and designed to welcome you to the community. There will be activities designed for the extroverted student who wants to actively engage, and there will be ways for the quiet connector to get a feel for the place. If you're the person who prefers to take it in on your own, there will be a welcoming space for you to sit back and observe. Orientation should help you feel like you belong or at least like you're starting to belong.

Your orientation will likely begin with an acknowledgment of the land. To identify the Traditional Territories on which your university sits, please consult the native-land.ca website. Use the geolocator to pinpoint your location and learn more about the land beneath your feet.

In the spirit of connecting, and going forward in a good way, let's talk about how to begin your journey on campus.

STUDENT STORY

I was surprised to experience an actual grand entry on my first day. In my culture, a grand entry symbolizes the beginning of a great journey, which really is how this all feels. It's been emotional.

– TRACEY

INDIGENOUS LANDS AND GREETINGS

Indigenous traditions invite us to introduce ourselves starting with our connection to the land: where we were born and who we are related to. In this spirit, please allow me to introduce myself again. My name is Janet Miller (née Browne), and I was born and raised on the Traditional Lands of the Mississaugas of the Credit First Nations, in a place that is now known as Oakville, Ontario. My ancestors were settlers who came from England, Scotland, and Ireland, with the exception of my great-great-grandmother.

My great-great-grandmother was an Indigenous woman. When her marriage was recorded, she was listed only as "Odawa woman" alongside her husband (whose name was fully recorded). Her memory has been passed down to me by my nanna, my mother, and my aunt. Other than these whispers, I was raised to honour the history of only my colonial ancestors and to feel proudly Canadian. I was not raised to understand how my settler ancestors attempted to eradicate the First Peoples of this land.

As I listen to (or deliver) a land acknowledgment, I try to honour all of my ancestors but especially my Odawa grandmother. Her memory encourages me to face the truth about continued colonization and to act to stop these injustices. She reminds me to reconnect with the land, remember the truth of the past, and go forward in a good way.

Orientation Essentials

Tour Around

Locate your classes, find the library, and take note of where you can eat or hang out. Having a general understanding of where things are will help you feel at home on campus. Organized tours might happen in the summer via video streaming or 3D modelling, and small tours might be organized right before classes begin. If you'd rather not go along for a formal tour, ask a returning student to show you around – it's a great way to start a connection with someone new. Knowing where you're going will significantly lower your stress levels on the first days of class.

STUDENT STORY

The tour was the best. Finding my classes helped me to feel more confident on my first day. I got this! – SAMIYAH

Memorize Your Student Number

Also known as your Student ID or an SN, your student number is a unique identification that links you to your school. You needed this number for registration, but you'll also need it for all kinds of other things on campus. It's tied to your grades, campus services, and your transcript. Log the number into your phone and memorize it.

Get Your Campus ID Card

The longest wait during orientation will likely be for getting your campus ID card, which will include your student number and a photo. Some schools allow you to email or upload your own photo, others will insist you show up for a brief photo shoot. Unlike most IDs, in this one, you can smile. Comb your hair and try to go early to avoid the crowds. Or go in the middle of the day, embrace the longer lines, and enjoy the chance to make small talk with some of your future friends.

Your card will give you access to printers, photocopiers, the library, an email account, the gym, and services such as counselling, career services, tutoring, and advising. You might need it to get into the bar. Keep it close. Carry it with you.

Look for Swag and Free Food
Get something that has your university logo on it. Could be a hoodie, a toque, a binder, a lanyard, or a T-shirt. You'll see a ton of choices in the university bookstore, and you'll likely get a bag of swag (Stuff We All Get) when you attend orientation. University branding is often given out freely at the beginning of term to help build school spirit and enhance your sense of community. Free merch is generally great, but if there are strings attached – beware. I've heard stories about credit card companies luring students in by offering free food and T-shirts.

STUDENT STORY

Appreciated the free food. Lots going on all week. – NATHANIEL

Free meals or snacks will be available throughout orientation, but be on the lookout for free food options throughout the year. Many schools offer a free breakfast program and discounted ways to get fruits and veggies.

Find Another Program Newbie and One Senior Student
Throughout your orientation sessions, you'll be thrown together with other new students. Some of these people will be in your program. Take notice and you'll find that familiar faces start to stand out. Meeting one person who shares a class with you will make going to class a bit easier at the beginning of term.

Somewhere in your orientation sessions – online, at an event, or while lining up for coffee – you're going to meet student volunteers. All of these students have some experience at your university. They're generally nice humans, donating their time to help newbies out. Ask questions, and see if you can find a volunteer who is also in your program. A second-year nursing student will have a lot of great advice for fresh students entering the program. The same is true for all majors. Getting an insider view of your program will be helpful.

If you're living in residence, then you're going to be paired up with a senior student automatically. These students are called RAs – residence assistants – sometimes called dons, residence advisors, or floor fellows. They'll have knowledge of the school and a million pieces of wisdom to share with you. They're also hired to help build community and are invested in making your first year a success.

It's easy to get overwhelmed with details at your orientation events, but there will always be someone around to help you. Almost all universities have tutors, counsellors, nurses, physicians, learning strategists, career advisors, peer mentors, Indigenous centres, queer spaces, clubs, societies ... the list goes on and on. All universities will be full of people willing to offer support. They'll be able to connect you with the help you need.

Your best resource? This will likely be other students. Throughout orientation events, look for familiar faces. Find a great guide and possibly a great friend.

Safety, Security, and Services

Your orientation sessions will also provide information about essential resources designed to support a healthy undergraduate experience. Look for those that will reduce barriers, address systemic racism, build meaningful relationships, and provide venues for student advocacy.

Accessibility Services

These professionals support students with documented disabilities (including learning, mobility, vision, hearing, learning, attention, neurological, or psychological diagnoses and chronic medical conditions). If you're coming into university with a diagnosis, or if you think that you have a condition that is affecting your learning but you haven't yet been diagnosed, then connect with your Accessibility Office right away. There are many resources available to support your success in university. For other resources, check out the provincial guidebooks available online (e.g., Alberta Transition Planning Guide, Ontario Transition Resource Guide).[1]

Read Your Student Conduct Guide

Moving into university means you'll have a lot more freedom and choice. Your university wants to keep you safe throughout these adventures. Inside and outside of the classroom you will be expected to conduct yourself responsibly and show respect for the people and places around you. Every school has a student code of conduct that outlines not only your responsibilities but also your rights. It's worth reading, especially if you need more clarification about what constitutes plagiarism in the university environment.

No one is ever entitled to anyone's time, attention, or body – regardless of the relationship we're in, or the desire we have for another person. Ultimately, sex is a reciprocal, mutually pleasurable exchange, and our goal should *always* be to ensure that the people we're giving sexual attention to are feeling good about what's going on.

– SAM PEARSON, director, Sexual Assault Centre, University of Alberta

Zero Tolerance for Sexual Violence

Your university will value everyone's boundaries and identities, and as part of that community you are expected to understand consent and practice it in your personal and romantic relationships. Please remember that being drunk is not an excuse to violate the student code of conduct or commit a crime, and you can expect to still be held accountable for your actions. If you have been affected by dating, domestic, or sexual violence, know that it's not your fault. Sexual assault centres and student counselling services are available on campus to help.

How do you know if your sexual actions are wanted? You don't know unless you ask and, under the law, you must ask for (and receive) the person's permission. Your university will have a definition of sexual consent that looks a lot like this one from Ryerson University:

Consent is defined as the active, ongoing, informed and voluntary agreement to engage in physical contact or sexual activity. Consent cannot be given by someone who is incapacitated (such as by drugs or alcohol), unconscious, or otherwise unable to understand and voluntarily give consent.[2]

WHAT IS SEXUAL ASSAULT?

According to Dalhousie University's sexual violence policy, available on its website,[3] sexual assault is

- any form of unwanted, forced, or coerced sexual activity, including kissing, fondling, touching, and any kind of intercourse, that is done onto the Member of the University Community or Visitor without their consent; or

- any attempts or threats, by an act or a gesture, to force sexual activity onto the Member of the University Community or Visitor.

Forcing or coercing someone to touch you sexually is also sexual assault.

Sexual assault can happen to anyone, of any gender. It may be committed by someone you know (spouse, partner, family member, roommate, date) or by a stranger. Acquaintance sexual assault is more common than assault by a stranger. Acquaintance sexual assault often occurs when one or more of the parties involved has been drinking or using drugs; in these circumstances, inhibitions and communication skills are diminished. Using alcohol or drugs does not excuse sexual assault, nor does it make the person assaulted in any way responsible for the assault.

Still have questions? Check out the video "Consent: It's Simple as Tea" on YouTube.[4] Also look to your university for policies, procedures, and supports.

Campus Safety

In addition to all of the above, your university will also have a security team on-site to help keep you and the campus safe. Instead of walking alone at night, you can use the Safe Walk program or ask a security guard to support you in that way. Information technology (IT) service is responsible for cybersecurity issues while student services handle all kinds of issues or problems. At a higher level, your university will have an emergency response team trained to lead faculty and students through unexpected crises. Most safety work happens behind the scenes, but you can support it by reading your student conduct guide, participating in fire drills, and downloading the campus app.

Recreational Facilities

Most universities have a swimming pool, running track, and gym facilities, and usually full-time students are automatically members. Personal training sessions, exercise classes, certification courses, or recreational lessons are also likely available (though perhaps at an additional cost). Find out what your university offers, then join a workout challenge, sign up for a rec class, or go for solo workouts. These are great ways to relieve stress and meet other people.

Other Student Services

Rather than introduce you to a long list of student services now, I include a list at the end of this book (and, yes, it's indeed long). For now, just know that your university website also includes all the details of what's available on campus. Look under the "On Campus" tab or under "Student Life," "Student Affairs," or "Student Services." If in doubt, please talk with your academic advisor and tell them what you need. I'm sure they'll point you towards the appropriate service, and that resource will most likely be free, on campus, and easy to access.

The Calendar

Every school publishes a calendar of need-to-know dates. When do you register for Fall classes? When do you have to pay fees? Is there a withdrawal date? When do exams begin and end? You'll need to know these dates – find them online by searching the campus website for critical dates, ask your advisor, or check at the campus bookstore.

Setting Up for Class

On your first day, don't fall into the trap of bringing a thirty-five-pound book bag – bring only what you need: limit yourself to a wallet, a water bottle, and laptop or a few pens and a binder or notebook.

The Course Outline, Otherwise Known as the Syllabus

You'll receive your course outlines on the first day of class. These documents are key to your success at university. Each course has one, and each one is unique. A course syllabus is a contract that explains everything that will be expected of you in the class. It details how many exams, papers, or quizzes will be required, how much they count towards your final grade, and their due dates. It outlines everything that is expected of you in the class – what counts for grades and what doesn't.

If you want to give yourself an advantage in your studies, get a wall calendar that outlines the four months of the semester. Using your course outlines, plot out every deadline you're facing. We'll talk later about how to cope with the pinch points, those clusters of due dates affectionately known as November Nightmares and March Madness. For now, just get those exams and paper deadlines loaded into a calendar where you can keep track of them easily.

Textbooks

Some students say textbooks aren't necessary; nearly all professors say they're essential. Most course outlines detail which texts are required reading, and many classes also include a "recommended reading" list. Don't make any purchases until you've gone to class, heard the professor's opinion on what to buy, and confirmed you're taking the course. Once you're committed to the class, look for opportunities to buy used books (many students sell their books at

QUICK TIP ⚡

An online electronic calendar might be okay, but a wall calendar that shows the four-month semester all in one glance is best. Smaller calendars that fit in your backpack are also good, but try to get one that at least allows you to see an entire month at once. You'll find that deadlines have a harder time sneaking up on you when you can see the whole picture.

the end of term). Check in with upper-year students about which books were top priority and think about your long-term plans. If the course covers a topic you're hoping to major in, having textbooks written by experts in the field will likely be worth the investment. If you don't want to buy a book, you'll likely find copies available to borrow from the library. A word of caution: If the library's edition or the used copy of the textbook is not the same as the one assigned, you'll have to do some searching to make sure you're reading the right pages or sections. Since access to these books is free, you may find they're in demand or available only for a few hours at a time.

The Library

The library is another key place you'll need through the year. Some universities have one main library space while others have specialized libraries peppered all over campus. Many students find these buildings intimidating, and sometimes library spaces, systems, and ways to access information aren't obvious or intuitive. I assure you, though, once inside you'll find librarians and expert staff who will be willing to help you. What makes these spaces special are the people who are always there to assist you (they're there to answer your questions), so when you get that first paper or assignment – go and ask for help at the library desk. All libraries have online resources, and some also offer workshops, individualized learning services, and technology loans or support.

Key Messages

Orientation can be exciting and overwhelming, so make sure to do the following to get the most out of it:

☆ Find branded swag.

☆ Take a tour.

☆ Know your student number and get an ID card.

☆ Eat some free food.

☆ Say hello to one other new student and find a senior student in your program.

☆ Get a hold of the student conduct guide.

☆ Understand consent and practise it in your relationships.

☆ Find the gym.

☆ Get in touch with Accessibility Services if you need their support.

☆ Send an email to your advisor, and meet them before the term ends.

☆ Skim the student services list at the back of this book or on your campus website.

☆ Read your course outlines.

☆ Set up a wall calendar of deadlines.

☆ Purchase your textbooks and some school supplies (not many) and rent a locker.

☆ Find the library.

STUDENT TIP 📌

Since we don't have overdue penalties in libraries in Japan, I was shocked to discover that this is common in Canada. There were no visible indications or signs of warning about the penalty system on my receipt or in the library. When I was charged five dollars for being late by one day, I was upset. My family is already paying a lot for my education. I am trying very hard (maybe too much) to limit my expenses. Thankfully, she granted an exemption in the end. But it was a hard experience to go through. – MIZUKI OSHITA, undergraduate student, Mount Royal University, from Kobe, Japan

EARLY DAYS
ON CAMPUS

How long will it take to feel at home in this place?
Can I shake off my high-school identity here?
What strategies can I use right now to help me adjust to university life?

MAYA ANGELOU, the American poet and civil rights activist, said that *who you are is enough*: so long as you're real with yourself, then you're going to feel at home everywhere you go. This is beautiful and true but also incredibly hard to do when you first come onto campus.

Universities are huge spaces, and you're going to feel a bit lost until you figure out how to get around, where things are, and who works where. You're going to need to walk around, check things out, and learn about this place. Give yourself a bit of time, and adopt new strategies to adapt. They'll help you feel like you belong.

STUDENT STORY

Samiyah grew up in the city. She loves magazines – the real ones you can hold in your hand, with the shiny paper that slips through your fingers. She went to an inner-city high school and had decent grades, despite some exploration with drinking and making retro rap videos. With that phase behind her, she was looking forward to a fresh start in university. She decided to wear a hijab and has been learning more about her faith. She was accepted into several journalism programs but decided to stay local so she could live at home and save money. She found that many of her high-school friends didn't know how to respond to her now that she's wearing a headscarf. She was called fake by some and shunned by others. Breaking out of her old identity was complicated by what others

thought she "should" be doing, but for Samiyah the journey towards being real with herself felt worth the effort. The turmoil of not being accepted helped her to clarify what she believed in and why.

Walking around with your eyes on your phone and your thoughts stuck on your worries isn't going to help you feel connected. New phases of life require adaptation. It's time to revise old habits and adjust to university life.

According to research led by Charles Spielberger and his colleagues Eric Reheiser and Laura Starr from the University of South Florida, being curious motivates exploratory behaviour and improves problem solving.[1] Curiosity is a psychological vital sign that can be used to reduce anxiety and worry. Showing interest in something (or someone) puts you in the perspective of an observer; once you've adopted this perspective, you'll be more likely to notice things, get outside of yourself, have a sense of wonder, and see the possibilities.

Find Places Where You Belong

Space is an important part of belonging. When you first come to campus, the buildings and walkways will feel foreign. Signs might point the way, but it feels awkward standing there reading them.

I encourage new students to explore their campus. You need to know where your classes are, how to get to and from the bar or coffee shop, and how to get to and from the library (even if you're not ready to use it yet).

Tuck a book under your arm, put your phone away, and hold your head up so you look like you know where you're going, and walk around. Explore inside and outside. Check out your buildings and others. Look for doorways and places to sit. Check out staircases, hallways, paths, and green spaces. Walk until you've found at least two places to eat, two water bottle filling stations, and a few bathrooms.

Sociologists have found that it's important to have at least three places in your life where you feel you belong. Home might be one of them, but we need other places where we can also be at ease. In the book *The Naked Roommate*, Harlan Cohen puts this idea into practice on campus, stating that students need to find three places where they can hang out.[2] This is an idea worth exploring. The goal here is to claim some of this space as your own so you don't feel like you're just visiting.

Here's how you do it:

1. Look for places that suit you. Your three places might all be in one building or spread out across campus – that's going to depend on where your classes are and the activities you're interested in. Choose public areas that are easy to get to. Later in your studies, you may want to book study rooms in the library, but for now, stick with open areas.

Look for places as you walk into campus each day. All universities have places to hang out in. It might be a table where you can have a coffee or lunch, or a sofa where you can check your phone, nap, or review your notes. Some students prefer the comfy chairs in the library by the windows along the south wall; others prefer the quiet nook up on the top floor where almost no one walks by. There will be a lounge in the student union building, a bench outside, and cubicles somewhere down the hall.

Activity-based locations also count. The gym, for example, could become one of your places. A track to run on or a space to do crunches and deadlifts can become places where you belong. You may need a walking space that takes about a half hour to stroll or run through. This will become a place where you can go when you need to decompress, think things through, or vent. You can't always rely on someone to pick up your desperate phone call, but you can rely on sidewalks being available and paths being open 99 percent of the time. Whatever you choose, these spaces should be places where you can relax. Try out a few, and you'll soon see which ones feel best.

STUDENT STORY

Because she loves sunshine, Samiyah eventually found that she preferred to read outside, and one of her favourite places became the

front steps by the fountains. She enjoyed the moisture in the air and found that the constant swishing of the water helped to keep her mind on task. When the weather was poor, she found that tables in the far corner of the cafeteria were great, especially ones by the windows.

2. Store your stuff. If you have a locker, use it. Drop off your books or whatever bulky stuff (skateboard, parka, or Chem text) you may have. If you're in a cold climate, store a lighter coat and a pair of comfy shoes to wear indoors. If you drive to campus, dump your baggage in your car.

If you don't have storage space on campus, then make sure one of your three places provides enough room to gear down and spread out.

3. Test them out. Go to your spaces a few times each day to see what the traffic is like and how quiet or vibrant the atmosphere gets. Notice the people coming and going and consider whether this place gives you the social opportunities you're craving or the privacy you feel you need. Try the spaces out on different days of the week, and use them for different types of activities. Some spaces will help you focus on your work; others will provide you with entertainment, challenges, or distractions.

If you have a crappy day and need to take a mental break before heading on to the next thing, your autopilot navigation system will take you to one of these spaces, where you can do what you need to feel better. For the first few weeks, while new friendships are taking shape, these spaces will give you a sense of belonging and a place to purposefully go. These kinds of planned spaces make campus feel more like home.

Eventually, you'll include new spaces – study halls, coffee shops, or pubs. Soon you'll notice student centres, clubs, and associations where you can get specific information; you'll join activities or contribute to the social fabric of the school. You'll find that these spots will become your new places to hang out.

Establish a Routine but Mix It Up

At first, everything's new, and everything looks unfamiliar. The first time you park on campus or get off the bus – walking down the halls, looking for the classroom, and checking the door number several times to make sure you're in the right place – it will all feel a bit surreal. Don't be surprised if you feel nervous. It's normal.

Establishing a routine will help you claim a space early on – where you'll sit in each class, which table you gravitate to in the cafeteria, which lot you'll choose to park in. These new patterns will help you feel secure in these unfamiliar surroundings, *but as soon as you feel at ease, mix it up again.* Meeting people and finding your place requires you to be alert and engaged.

To wake up your mind and activate your senses, make a conscious effort to do some of those routine things in different ways. Since we're talking about places and spaces here, I challenge you to break the status quo:

- Map three routes to get to class.
- Try sitting in a different seat in class, at least occasionally.
- Alternate which hand or shoulder you carry your bag with or on.
- Cross your legs or arms the other way.
- If you're taking classes from a distance, then create three working spaces where you can sit and log in.
- Brush your teeth with your non-dominant hand.
- Change your clothes as soon as you get home (a great stress-management tool).

Add variety into your world, and your brain will thank you for it. When we think intentionally about routines and brainstorm ways to keep them fresh, we prime our brains to manage complicated information. It keeps us on our toes.

Explore Your Identity or Revamp Your Image

You've likely been told that you're going to change a lot through university – and it's true. While you already have a solid idea of who you are, what you like to do, what you're good at, and who you're attracted to, and so on, you'll find that your identity will expand with exposure to new possibilities. You might know that you like biology but not know that you love cellular microbiology because you haven't had a chance to learn about it yet. Maybe you have hidden talents for event organization, a passion for anthropology, or amazing abilities in microeconomics. School will provide opportunities for new experiences, and by exploring those possibilities you'll develop a clearer picture of who you are.

In addition to intellectual development and expansion, university also provides the opportunity to reinvent your identity or revamp your image, if you want to. You get to update your look, shake off old nicknames, and outgrow that embarrassing thing you did back in Grade 9. For some, it will be their first chance to express their true self. Whether it's purple hair, advocating for authentic pronouns, or a new piece of ink, university may be the space to put your identity out there.

STUDENT STORY

Being queer in a small town is not for the faint of heart. I think I repressed most of my identity purely as a means to cope with loneliness. But all that changed when I got to university. The year *started* with the city's Pride Parade, and within a week I was part of the Queer Collective. The beauty of the people here amazes me.
– RENEE

University life is a time of exploration and experimentation, too – physical, spiritual, sexual, emotional, and intellectual. This time in your life is amazing in every sense of the word. It's also hard, confusing, and exhausting.

In many cultures, the drive to self-actualize (to achieve your full potential) and express your identity is thought to be hard-wired into our being. Identity expression is considered important for healthy development. It was Abraham Maslow, an American psychologist, who coined the term *self-actualization* in 1943, and he created a hierarchy of needs with it at the top.[3] He saw self-actualization as being part of our peak experience, noting that people tend to express and uncover their true selves once their other needs for food, shelter, safety, love, and self-esteem have been met.

Research by Deborah Coon has shown that much of Maslow's theory was based on what he learned from the Blackfoot way of life during a 1938 visit to Siksika First Nation. As Indigenous scholar Cindy Blackstock explains in her 2019 article on breath-of-life theory, many Indigenous cultures in North America value all of the needs Maslow presents but consistently speak of self-actualization as being first and fundamental, building the way for community actualization and cultural perpetuity.[4] How can we be of value to others if we don't first know ourselves and our purpose? Knowing yourself and then living authentically in line with your identity is a solid base. Your identity then becomes the foundation for everything else: healthy relationships, safety, food security, and self-esteem.

I don't know how you experience your drive to self-actualize right now, but I do know that you'll do a lot of this work throughout university. This process will involve your culture, values, and experiences in the past as well as the experiences you're about to have in school. I don't know where you come from or what led you to school, but I do know that you'll draw strength from those sources.

STUDENT STORY

After learning the academic flow, my biggest challenge was balancing two worlds. I had one foot on the concrete floor of the academic institution and the other foot bare, resting on the soil of my mother, trying to find my spirit's way home to heal.
– ANDREA HERON, Psychology, Mount Royal University Alumna

Let's acknowledge that coming to university represents different things to different students. You may be the first in your family to attend university, or maybe you're here because many relatives have already graduated from this particular place. You may distrust institutions or feel at ease within them. Students might feel on guard, relaxed, or freaked out as they enter campus. You may be here by choice, or perhaps you were pressured into attending. Regardless of your situation, finding ways to be at university on your own terms is going to be important to your success. To make school feel like your own, you have to explore the landscape. Making friends will take effort, but you'll find that there are a lot of events, systems, and people to support you.

Finding your way also means being open to the potential this new space offers. For students who are the first in their family to go to university, you might feel the enthusiasm of your relatives around you as a driver, or you might not be surrounded by people who understand your decision to pursue this kind of education. No two experiences are the same. Even if you're in the same program that your mom took, or the same residence your brother lived in, your experience will be unique. The players have changed, the décor has been updated (we hope!), and education has advanced in a way your family may not realize.

Give and Take, and Play the Long Game

Making a space your own also means contributing to it. Taking care of campus could be as simple as picking up a stray piece of garbage and recycling it or stopping to help someone who is lost in the halls. Once you feel at home, make an effort to welcome others. Consider volunteering next year for student orientation to help welcome the newbies to *your* university.

You belong here now. Rock it.

Through your studies, you'll find dozens of other ways to give back to your community. Some small, others substantial – all important. In 2019, I and my colleagues, Andrea Heron, Michelle Pidgeon, and Jennifer Ksionzena, interviewed alumni and learned that many learners felt compelled to bring their newly acquired knowledge and skills back to their communities for the benefit of the next generation. They highlighted the importance of seeing one's self as a vehicle for sharing understanding and for helping others to thrive. As you receive knowledge and wisdom, find ways to bring balance, pay it forward, and keep the circle moving.

A happy life has been linked with hedonistic experiences (like joy and pleasure), but a good life is broader and encompasses things such as satisfaction, contributing to a greater good, and self-discovery. Aristotle, the Greek philosopher, spoke of eudemonic happiness, the kind of good life that comes from challenging work. It's the satisfaction that comes from building mastery and having a positive impact.

In school, I hope you have a wild time – enjoy yourself, laugh, express yourself, and explore the freedoms that come with being in this stage of life. You'll work harder than ever, struggle to figure things out, draw on resources (internal and external), and achieve things you never thought possible. Unlocking your potential and finding your career path are incredible feelings. You'll get to the point where you can see a future that is in line with your goals and values. Often that clarity comes from the tough stuff. From hard work. Trial and error. Persistence. It also comes from making efforts that are valuable – valuable to yourself and those around you.

As you think about your long game, you'll want to focus on your own goals (grades, grad, whatever), but you'll also want to look for ways to support others. Find causes that motivate you, identify issues that reflect your values, and explore potential solutions. You may decide to rise up in the face of injustice or to take a stand on an issue. Universities are places of debate and dialogue, inquiry and questioning. Making a meaningful contribution could mean taking the initiative, expanding on current work, solidifying efforts, or making something more sustainable. Whatever your legacy, you'll find it intensely satisfying and personally rewarding.

This won't come together in your first six weeks on campus – but over the next few years you'll find your way.

Key Messages

☆ The early days on campus can be intimidating. Finding your three places will help.

☆ Adopt an attitude of curiosity.

☆ Establish some routines to help you claim your space and navigate the campus.

☆ Walk around the campus – a lot. Explore. Doing this with another new student can be a great way to bond.

☆ Be prepared to discover more about yourself as you're exposed to new and different ideas.

☆ Self-actualization is an ongoing process, and it may be the foundation of our overall well-being.

☆ Get yourself some storage space: use a trunk organizer or get a locker. Walking lighter through the halls will help you feel at ease, and having a locker means you'll have a place to go.

☆ Although these are early days, start to notice ways that you might get involved with campus life. How might you contribute to making this a better place?

☆ Keep your eye on the long game – even in these early days.

FINDING YOUR PEEPS
AND SETTLING IN

Will the hype of September last?
Is it better to stick with old connections or break out into new crowds?
Am I the only one who's finding it hard to make friends?

FINDING YOURSELF? That's a lifelong process.

But finding your people? That needs to happen right away.

You won't realize how essential these university friendships are until they're in place.

Figuring out what you love, who you love, what you're great at – these are all things that evolve during this phase of your life – what researcher Jeffrey Arnett calls "emergent adulthood."[1] Adolescence is over, but you probably don't feel like an adult yet. Your university years will be among the best of your life – it's a time of freedom, choice, possibility, and independence. It's also a time of change and upheaval. You're mostly out of the pimples and hormone-spike stage, but maybe not quite. Some of you still have the last growth spurt to look forward to, and research says your brain will continue to grow until about the age of twenty-five. Cells are still forming, pathways are strengthening. While all this change is happening, you'll have to cope with wanting to procrastinate one moment and being impulsive the next. These emotional fluctuations won't necessarily make sense, and at times you'll feel confused about your capabilities, strengths, self-worth, and relationships. This is all normal. Finding people you relate to is going to help.

Of course, in class, you'll want to focus on the professors at the front of the room – and hopefully they'll teach you useful things in interesting ways.

However, you're also going to want to get to know the people around you. The person who sits beside you in the lab or lecture hall. Those who stand with you in line for coffee and those who take the same bus or train. You'll have classmates, maybe teammates, and roommates too. You really are in the process of making lifelong friends. The more people you get to know, even casually, the more at home you're going to feel in this space.

Sexually, you might find yourself exploring, having a good time, hooking up, or talking it up. There will be spaces and places on your campus that embrace diversity and the fluidity of all identities, gender, orientation, or otherwise. During these years, regardless of whether you're sexually active, you'll discover who you're attracted to, what turns you on, and what turns you off.

Many of you will make romantic connections during these university years. Some will fade quickly, others will last a lifetime. Look around. Smile at the people beside you and get to know who they are and what they're about. You never know when you're going to make one of those amazing connections.

The people who work on campus will be part of your journey too – the person at the parking office, the trainers at the gym, or the barista at your favourite coffee spot. Knowing and being known in the community is going to help you to feel at ease in this place. You're a regular here, and you're going to get to know the faces behind the counters and in the offices.

These connections will be helpful, but you still need friends your own age – people who understand your experiences and get what you're about. One of my favourite generation-gap stories happened a few years ago in our student union building. A member of our university security team was looking at a social media channel run by students and saw a post "We're Having Sex – third floor, Wyckham."

Freaking out, the officer summoned the team and ran to the third floor of our student union building (Wyckham House) to break it up. Imagine their surprise when they found a group of students casually hanging out at tables, streaming videos and working on a school project. The officers were mortified when they were told that We're Having Sex was the name of Michael Callahan's 2013 award-winning short film and that the post was just a call-out to a film class study group.

Shared memories like this one are what make the university years among the best of our lives. According to the students who've gone ahead of you, there are many ways to foster friendships and build those connections. Consider these ideas.

Look for People Who Share Your Interests

To find your peeps, look for friends who not only connect with your music but also share your other interests, beliefs, and sense of humour. Your student union will have clubs of all varieties: Muslim student associations, queer student groups, Black student networks, and antiracism coalitions. You'll be able to connect through international student societies, Christian fellowships, and Indigenous cultural centres.

Through first year, you'll likely create a variety of connections with people who are like you in a variety of ways. Maybe you'll fall into a group to study and laugh into the night with, or you'll connect with one or two friends who will hold your hair back while you pray to the porcelain gods, stick with you through a breakup, or pick you up when your bicycle gets stolen or your car breaks down. You'll likely call on high-school friends first, but as time goes on you'll add others to your inner circle.

I hope you find a combination of friends – some who have similar ideas and some who think differently, some who share your program of study and career path and others who share (and stretch) your interests in and outside of school. Sometimes you'll find a combination of career and fun in one person, or one group of friends, but we often start with the professional and move into the personal. It takes time to build real relationships, but you'll slowly build that social network of support that every student needs.

Making the switch from high school or CEGEP into university is a kind of cross-cultural shift. The transition is even more complex when you're moving from a small town to a city, from a reserve to an urban centre, or from home into residence.

Reach Out through Images and Symbols

Covering your body or your backpack with symbols that reflect who you are or what you stand for can be another way to initiate a connection with like-minded individuals. Your personal style of clothing and footwear will make a statement that reflects your identity, or you could be more blatant, choosing to wear symbols or slogans that carry a particular meaning.

Sometimes we wear a symbol purely for aesthetic fashion, but most individuals choose things with intention. Look around at the people walking by or sitting next to you and notice how they reveal their identity in subtle and obvious ways. Silk hijabs or silver crosses, rainbow flag or semicolon tattoos, a #MeToo button or a lavender rhino? Band logos, memes, even avatars – all these things send a message that the wearer hopes will be heard. Look for symbols that are meaningful to you and use those as a starting point for conversations. Chances are you'll have more than just that symbol in common.

Don't Treat University Like it's a Movie ...

Most of us know what it's like to be in a movie theatre. We enjoy sitting in front of the big screen and being absorbed in action scenes and storytelling. Watching movies is part of our cultural norm, and our thirst for entertainment is reinforced through our electronic devices. It's not therefore surprising that many students approach classrooms looking to be entertained. (They are called lecture *theatres* after all.)

But going to a movie is a passive experience. Yes, you pick the film and buy a ticket, but once you're there, you just sit down and enjoy. Since it's awkward to arrive late, most people don't. Instead, you arrive a few minutes ahead of the show to get to your seat. You likely watch the movie in the company of others, but it's not an interactive activity, and you don't usually talk with people you don't already know. Mostly, you sit back and absorb what's coming at you, and then you leave. You might talk about the movie with your friends, maybe even reference it for years to come, but you don't usually hang around the theatre once the show is over.

Going to university has some similarities. You choose the location (through your application and acceptance), you certainly have to pay to attend, and lectures should capture your attention and provide some entertainment value. But attending school should be an active experience. Students who mistake university for a movie theatre don't talk with people in their classes, and they leave as soon as the lecture is over. This is especially true for commuter students who live at home and for students who pack work hours tightly around their class schedules.

When you treat school like a movie theatre, it's mostly the social opportunities you'll miss out on. Making friends in university takes effort. Try to arrive early and talk with the people around you. I know that in the first weeks of September, many students avoid this by aiming to arrive on campus just in time for the bell (only there are no bells in university). Because if you go too early you risk sitting in the awkward vortex of pre-class silence. Arrive after the class has started and face the possibility of being mortified as you walk in late or missing out on the class altogether. Although most professors would strongly prefer you arrive late rather than not show at all, many students worry about the disruption they'll cause if they walk in a few minutes after the lecture has started.

Honestly, don't worry about it – just go in.

If you treat your class like going to a movie, you'll be inclined to sit passively through the lecture and beeline out as soon as class is over. This is often just the way it is early on, and that's okay. It's strange to hang around campus when there's no real reason to yet, and it's painfully awkward to strike up a conversation with someone for the first time, or to walk into a crowded food court where you don't know a soul. Eventually, you'll scan classrooms and cafeterias for friendly faces rather than empty seats, but this takes time. You can only do what you can do with what you've got, right now, at this point in time. Next week will be different (and likely better). If you're feeling awkward right now, that's okay. In a month you won't.

STUDENT STORY

It took months to feel like I could just hang around on campus. It changed when I had to meet my lab partners outside of class to get a project done, and then we joined the Chemistry Students' Society together and got more involved. These friendships gave me a reason to arrive early for class and to stay through the day.
– MATEO

... but it's Not Just a Party Either

So, we don't want to think of university like a movie we passively sit back and watch, but be careful, though. Looking too intently for connection can sometimes drive us in directions that get us off track. This happened with Jaren, who jumped into the social scene early and hard. He wanted to make friends, have a stellar time, and party. Academically, he had great potential. His high-school grades were strong, and he got into a program that was envied by many. Jaren joined a frat house, where he got to know people from all over. He couldn't walk around campus without seeing someone he knew. Terrific? Yes. But it was also awful in that he could always find someone who wasn't studying – someone that he would then skip class and hang out with. Hanging out (a.k.a., shooting hoops, gaming, drinking) became the dominant theme of his friendships, overshadowing class, studying, work, and making career connections.

Are you surprised to hear that his first term ended badly? It was true that Jaren made some real lifelong friends from his fraternity, but the other connections were simply surface acquaintances, people to hang out with but not people he could count on. For his classes, well, he didn't fail everything, but he failed some, and he was put on academic warning for the Winter term. Because he had to repeat some of his prerequisites, he fell out of sync with his cohort. This was not a complete disaster, but it wasn't the kind of semester he had wished for either. Second term brought more success – Jaren focused his social life on the campus bar night (Tuesday) and the frat house on weekends. He stopped skipping classes and made more connections with people in his program. By the end of the first year, he was back in good academic standing and on top of his game. He went on to graduate with honours and became a leader in his field. If he ever had the chance to address a first-year class, he'd tell them that he had to learn the hard way that university isn't just a party.

Think of University as a Bike Ride

Instead of thinking of university as a big party or as a passive form of edutainment, perhaps it makes sense to think of it as a long bike ride. If you know how to cycle, you'll remember that it's awkward until you get the hang of it. And so it is with student life.

Newbies are focused on their feet, on those shoes that pinch, and on the uncomfortable seat. They nervously struggle to find balance, and almost everyone gets better (and better) with practice. With experience, you don't wobble, the ride is smooth, and you rarely give your feet a second thought. You may glide in places, but a longer ride requires you to be active. It takes effort, and sometimes the conditions are gruelling. You'll have hills to climb and sharp turns to navigate, and you'll feel accomplished after each of those challenges. When you're done, you'll feel proud not only because of how far you went but also because of the experiences you had along the way. As cheesy as it sounds, the journey counts as much as the destination.

Where to Find Your People

How you get involved with others will be driven by who you are, where you live, and what you're interested in.

In a research study looking at barriers and supports for undergraduate students, successful alumni said that what you're involved with isn't what matters. It's more about how you're involved. Their feedback reflected engagement in many micro-moments. For example, when you're in class – make eye contact, smile, and be curious about who is around you. If you're in line at the Tim Horton's, say hello to the person next to you. If you're awkwardly waiting for class to begin, consider asking your neighbour a question. The more involved you are in these mini-interactions, the more involved you'll feel with the macro of campus life. Challenge yourself to smile at two strangers today.

I recommend joining your program society and one student club or intramural team. The first will look good on your résumé (it builds professional capacity and shows commitment), and the others will support your interests in life beyond school. Both provide opportunities to build fantastic friendships.

Here's a bit more about these possibilities and others.

Your Student Union

Student unions (sometimes called students' associations, federations, or councils) play an important role in the lives of students. Along with tuition, you've likely paid a student union fee to support advocacy and enhance student life. To support connection, your student union will house spaces for clubs and activities; it will organize student events, launch advocacy initiatives, and offer hundreds of ways to volunteer and get involved. There's usually a student union building with food vendors, lounge spaces, and a campus bar. Your fees go towards supporting service areas, too, including peer-support drop-in centres, a clubhouse, queer-positive spaces, and perhaps a legal clinic, fresh food market, or multicultural centre. If you're feeling lonely and want to meet other students, go to your student union office and ask for their advice.

Clubs

Student clubs are usually connected to the student union, and they're open to everyone. Look for interest-based clubs, activity clubs, and social groups. Maybe you're interested in joining a group that stands for tradition (such as a fraternity) or something more recreational (such as the ski club). There will things like knitting clubs, Buddhist meditation clubs, and social justice advocacy groups. You may find you connect with the Jewish Hillel Network or an Islamic students' association. Board-game clubs that go beyond chess are popular, along with cooking clubs (free food?) and improv groups. Go to the campus club fair, and you'll likely find hundreds of options to consider. Some universities list their clubs by category on the website or in alphabetical order. It's worth reading through the list to get a sense of what's out there. Whether it's knitting or debating, surfing or spoken word, there's going to be a club for you. If not... you always have the option to start one.

STUDENT STORY

I took a big risk in September, and I posted a comment on our class discussion board announcing that I wanted to form a study group. Four people responded, and after a few weeks, we were sitting together and meeting regularly. We aced the class, and those crazy kids became my closest friends. – BRAE

Societies

Many departments have clubs or student societies, such as the Philosophy Society, the Math Club, or Anthropology Students' Association. They're only open to students in those programs. Joining these groups will give you a chance to meet people with similar interests and career goals. You'll also find opportunities for leadership over time, and you'll be linked to a community of upper students and faculty too. Most societies have a faculty member who serves as a mentor, so that's another way to build connections. Later, this person might be able to write you a letter of reference for a job or a scholarship while providing some career guidance along the way.

Also, be on the lookout for pre-professional clubs or societies. They're open to a wider range of undergraduate students who share a career interest, such as the Pre-Med Club or the Pre-Law Club. These types of academic societies link you into a local (and perhaps national) network of like-minded peers, and they may connect you with mentors or future employers. In addition to making friends, you'll be making significant career connections. Be sure to add societal memberships onto your résumé.

Virtual Groups and Social Media Connections

Search online for university or college groups that match your demographic. For example, look for *Psych Undergrads, UBC first year,* or *Laurentian History Majors.* Searching for your expected graduation year – e.g., *McMaster Class of 'XX* – can also be fruitful. Some institutions have Reddit threads, Instagram feeds, and specialized apps too. Try engaging through those forums, and see who you find. You never know – you might meet someone that you have a few classes with.

Indigenous Centres

Indigenous student centres offer a relaxed, welcoming, supportive space where you can feel connected with a community. In addition to connecting with other students, you'll likely have opportunities to meet Elders and work with supportive staff in ways that improve your academic and personal well-being. Cultural events will be held throughout the year to support First Nations, Inuit, and Métis students, but all members of the campus community are welcome to join in. Once you begin hanging out in these spaces, you'll be sure to notice familiar faces and make connections.

Intramurals

A few years back I asked a bunch of student leaders, "Knowing what you know now, what advice would you give to first-years?" Most students surprised me by saying they would recommend joining intramurals.[2] Intramurals are recreational sports leagues that provide an outlet for friendly competition and a lot of social connection. There are leagues for students of different ability levels, so even if you're not especially good at a sport, you'll find people to play with. Students say that intramurals are a hilarious way to relieve stress, stay active, and meet new people. At my university, there's intramural soccer, floor hockey, and inner-tube water polo (true story!). Look at the recreation homepage or google *intramurals* to find out what's on offer at your school.

STUDENT TIP 📌

Kaylene McTavish is currently the New Student Orientation coordinator at Mount Royal University, but back in 2013 she was entering into the last year of her undergraduate degree. Having just completed a term as president of the Students' Association, I asked her to give some advice to first-year students. Her video response included this advice: "Knowing what I know now, being a fifth-year student at Mount Royal, this place has become my home, my community, my life. I would tell myself to enjoy every single minute. I'd tell myself to challenge myself when I didn't want to, and try all those things that scared me. And never look back, only forward. I would tell myself to start networking from the beginning because you never know who you're going run into in the future and who you're going to want to be friends with or who you're going to need as a resource. Networking is so important. I would tell myself to utilize every single resource that I have access to. And that student life is the best life, and [university] can be can be the best time of your life, if you choose it to be."[3]

Embrace Diversity

Working with a team of undergraduate researchers, we asked students about their views on student engagement and to describe qualities of "good university citizens." All participants talked about the importance of involvement, spending more time on campus, and making a positive contribution to university life. When you're active on campus you'll soon know who people are, where to find the free food, and where to get a late-night coffee. You'll also create solid friendships and feel a sense of belonging on campus. You'll no longer feel like a visitor. University will be your home.

There is a large body of research that links student engagement with academic success. Students who get involved with university life are more likely to succeed in their classes. These students also have high rates of degree completion. For example, when we looked at the long-term impact of student leadership roles on our campus, we found that across a ten-year period, the graduation rate of our residence advisors was nearly 100%.[4] Finding a way to be involved with your campus is going to be fun, but it's also going to help you succeed academically.

It's a big place, with a lot of people, and whether you're sporty, creative, or geeky, you're going to find others who are like you. You're also going to find a whole lot of others who are not like you – and this might be one of the best parts of being a student. You'll meet people from various backgrounds and cultures, people with similar interests but also with different points of view. At some point, you may find yourself questioning everything you've believed in. Maybe you'll become aware of all the privileges you have, or you'll become concerned about world issues. University will open your mind to variety and variation, expansion and pluralism. It's terrific, but also terrifying. Processing it together with classmates and friends will help you to find your people and deepen your connections. Universities are supposed to be places of protest, innovation, curiosity, and contemplation. Embrace the opportunity to embrace diversity.

Participants in our citizenship study said they saw opportunities to be engaged at several levels. You don't need to run for student council or initiate a program to be active on your campus. Start with attending activities. Go to a free lecture at lunch, listen in on a debate, pause to enjoy the "open mic night" at the pub or listen to a banned book reading at the library. It might be strange to go to these things on your own, but if you do you'll soon recognize familiar faces at these events – others who share your interests and people who might be real friend material. Hang out enough, and you'll find your people. They might not "look" like you, or they might come from different sides of the proverbial tracks, but you'll soon see that bonding occurs over common interests, not common backgrounds. This is part of the magic of university life.

STUDENT STORY

A film and media student came in for support because she felt alone in her program. The classes were interesting, but she wasn't connecting with other students. She wasn't being invited to social activities or study groups, and on top of that, she had just broken up with her girlfriend – a good decision for her but one that left her feeling extra lonely and out of sorts. School was so awkward that she found herself thinking of quitting, even though her marks were quite good.

In counselling sessions, we evaluated her reasons for continuing in school and reflected on her motivations for dropping out. We normalized and supported that feeling of loneliness that comes from ending a relationship and also that awkward feeling of not being included in the group. We looked at her assumptions – that she was being left out – and examined the evidence to see if she was correct (were there parties she wasn't being invited to?). As she began to look more closely at the situation, she found that she didn't really know what she was missing out on – she just knew that she felt a craving for connection that she wasn't getting.

She decided to try something different: she took a stab at creating the community she was craving before she ditched the program. She decided to plan a class outing to something completely out of her comfort zone. The campus was hosting a Sex Toy Bingo event. Yup. Sex Toy Bingo. (It might be a thing at your university too.) She was surprised to find that a dozen of her classmates said they would go. Reporting back to me in our next session, she said the experience was hilarious. It broke the ice immediately, and there was no room to hide from talking about personal things. The group laughed a lot and left with a boatload of shared memories. They also had material for hundreds of inside jokes.

During the next class, when they burst out laughing in unison, she felt completely uplifted. She soon realized that these social connections were new to everyone in her cohort. She hadn't been left out of anything after all. There just hadn't been anything going on.

Determined to be inclusive, she then reached out to everyone in the class and kept organizing group events: restaurant outings, a hike, poker nights, and study meetings. Empowered with the ability to create what she felt was missing, she discovered that the possibility of dropping out was no longer on her radar. She had created the community she longed for.

Key Messages

☆ September is a lot of fun, but it also holds out some false promises. First year will not be full of beer tents, balloons, and community events. Soak it up the best you can. September is all about settling in and finding your people.

☆ Look for ways to connect with people who are like you.

☆ And look for ways to connect with people who are different from you.

☆ Strive to join a club, society, group, or coalition – meeting people is easy when you're united around a common activity or purpose.

☆ Pay attention to the symbols of identity that are all around you – and choose your own with intention.

☆ Don't treat going to university like you would going to a movie. You need to be an active participant, not a passive one. But university isn't just a party either. It's going to be fun, but you also need to focus.

☆ Students who are engaged in university life are more likely to succeed academically. They report more satisfaction with their university years, and they're more likely to graduate.

☆ Consider ways to connect, even if it's just in micro-moments.

☆ If you aren't getting the community you're craving, try creating it.

☆ If you're feeling lonely and want to connect with other students, go to your student union and ask how you can be involved.

THE CRASH
(A.K.A OCTOBER,
FIRST GRADES BACK)

Midterms crushed me – what can I do to recover?
What kinds of study strategies are required for university-level courses?
What if I failed my first test?

ASK ANY PERSON you know who has gone through first year, and they'll tell you that October is a crash zone. At universities across the country, the demand for counselling appointments swells about six weeks into the term. The fast friendships of orientation fade, roommate conflicts crop up, and long-distance relationships fall apart. It's the month when the weight of the courseload and time pressures get real. You may experience disappointment with your first set of midterm marks, and you might feel lonely. As much as September builds you up, October can take you down.

We all knew that going to university was going to be stressful, but you might be surprised by the emotional and physical toll of it all.[1] Acquiring knowledge and mastering skills takes intense effort, so maybe it's understandable that students feel stress. Of the 55,284 Canadian university students who responded to the National College Health Assessment (NCHA) survey,

- 88 percent reported feeling overwhelmed by all they had to do
- more than half (54 percent) said they felt exhausted (and not by physical activity) in the past two weeks alone
- 70 percent said they had felt very lonely over the past year
- over half (52 percent) said they felt so depressed that it was difficult to function (20 percent within the last two weeks).[2]

This is the stuff I hear about in my counselling office, and it gives me that behind-closed-doors view of university life. Your experience of university has a much better chance of being phenomenal once we address the factors that make students crash.

Types of CRASH Traps

You might not even be aware that you're crashing until you miss a paper deadline or fail an exam. Chances are there's nothing wrong with you – but there may be a whole helluva lot wrong with what you're doing. If that's the case, then you're doing what 35 percent of first-year students do – you're crashing in October. Let's identify the kind of crash that's happening and get you back on course.

C Is for Coasting

Many new students approach university as if it's an extension of high school. The fact that university courses start slowly reinforces this false sense of security. Why develop new study habits when the old ones seem to be working just fine? It might be that you're used to procrastinating and have done well without studying, or maybe you're the kind of student who likes to spend hours recopying their class notes to perfection. Whatever your style, chances are it worked through Grade 12, and it will likely carry you through the first few weeks of university.

But then things change.

University workloads gain momentum through September and pick up serious speed as October approaches. Students who are still coasting along on their high-school approach will have serious trouble steering through that turn. They crash into the workload wall and tumble into midterms unprepared.

To the student who bombs their first set of tests, I want to say – you're not alone. I'm confident we can get you back on track.

In Donnie's case, after failing his first major midterm exam, he realized that he really didn't know how to study. He had coasted on his intellect for years, and all through high school he really didn't need to put much effort into getting decent grades. He realized that the bar had been raised, and the stakes were high. Donnie went to talk with his professor about the failed test, and she directed him to some peer-support resources. The peer group was good. He met senior students who were getting paid to tutor first-years, and their tips and strategies actually made sense. He took his term papers to the learning centre and met with a professional learning strategist – a service he was thrilled to find was free and easy to access. The strategist taught him how to structure long answers to essay questions and gave him a few grammar tips. Donnie realized his short-answer approach wasn't on point, and having another set of eyes on it really helped. The next set of midterms went much better. He pulled his grades out of the fire, and once he created daily strategies that worked for him, he found he still had plenty of time to get out and have fun. He also felt more confident, which meant he was able to relax and be himself again.

R Is for Reactive

Drew came to my counselling office in mid-October. In tears, she described herself as being overwhelmed by deadlines and so, so very tired. She said it felt like she was running from one fire to the next with no time to process what was happening. She was pissed off at her roommates and her professors. Midterms were upon her, and she said she wasn't getting the help she needed. Feeling desperate, she came in for support.

What should Drew do? Drop a course? Change roommates? Complain to the dean? No. The answer (and the power) was in Drew. The goal was to switch Drew's approach so she could be proactive and responsive instead of reactive and chaotic. Not easy but totally doable.

Students who approach their studies as a series of things to react to feel exhausted, out of control, and under pressure all the time. Reactions are defensive, aggressive, spontaneous, unconscious, quick, and not well thought through – very useful if you're in an emergency situation, but ineffective if used as a daily strategy. Being reactive will make you feel like a slave to circumstance.

Merriam-Webster defines *reactive* as "occurring as a result of a stress or emotional upset."[3] Being reactive is not the way you want to manage your academic life. Your university studies are something you're going to want to be more in charge of, so I'm going to encourage you to approach the situation proactively. Be responsive instead of reactive. Responses follow from reasoning. They're guided less by emotion and more by logic. Responses give us choice, and choice gives us power. We have time to consider possible actions and to make thoughtful decisions about what to do next.

Reactive	Responsive
• Focused on getting immediate relief	• Focused on solving the problem or issue
• Short-term solution	• Long-term success
• Fast, unconscious actions; knee-jerk behaviour	• Slower, thoughtful, considerate actions
• Driven by emotions	• Driven by reason
• Heat of the moment	• Calm
• Lash out	• Reach out
• Unsupportive, aggressive	• Supportive, empathetic
• Take things personally, highly sensitive	• Do not take things personally, more objective
• I can't change this (stuck)	• I can improve this (empowered)
• Fight or defend	• Resolve or create
• Feel out of control	• Feel in control
• Scattered	• Centred
• Playing catch-up	• Two steps ahead
• Rushing	• Anticipating
• Burned out, rushed, tired	• Measured, sustainable, paced
• Vulnerable to giving up	• Likely to stick with it

Consider the kinds of situations university will throw at you: assignments and essays, tests and labs, roommate conflicts, and social opportunities. You might feel overwhelmed, pissed off, or scared, and that's okay. It's what you do next that matters. If you're quick to emotionally react, you might hide away in your room, give up, or blame others. Let off some of that emotional steam in a way that doesn't hurt you or anyone else, and then look at what you can do to change the situation.

Responding is a slower process, but the results will be superior. As much as you can, put yourself into the responsive mindset. Change the narrative from "This sucks" and "Poor me," to "What can I do to address this?," "What are my options?," "Who can assist me?," and "Where can I start?" You'll have a greater sense of control, and that sense of empowerment will help you succeed and get back on track.

A Is for Alone

Being introverted isn't a problem, but being isolated is. It's a strong sign of the October crash when you haven't been to classes and you're spending most of your time alone in your room. On that same NCHA survey we talked about earlier, more than two-thirds of students reported feeling very lonely over the past year, and over half said they felt so depressed that it was difficult to function. If your strongest relationship is with a device, then we have a problem. We need to get you engaged with university life.

Gabby was surprised to find that instead of thinking about midterms, she was thinking about home. At home, there was always something to do, or someone to call on. She'd been on a leadership council and volunteered for events, which helped her develop confidence. She had a close group of friends and plenty of activities. Despite long-distance calls with her best friends and a few weekend trips home, that life seemed like a million miles away to her now. In her heart of hearts, she wanted to drop out and head home.

How did she get to this place of despair when she'd been so excited to come to university? What did she do wrong?

TIPS FOR MANAGING HOMESICKNESS

Keep in mind that feeling homesick is normal and common.

Create a daily routine and try to stick with it. It adds rhythm to your day and provides a sense of direction and focus.

If you plan to visit home through the term, try to hold off until mid-October. Use those early weekends to connect with campus activities and engage with university life.

Invest time in making your new space feel comfortable. Put some pillows on your sofa, get a plant for your window, or hang pictures up.

Stay in touch with friends and family back home through video chats and phone calls. Keep them up to date on what's happening in your life. Keep photos of people you love where you can see them.

Strive to make connections with local students who can show you the town.

Aim to share your holiday traditions with others from your university campus. Being together in times of celebration can help us feel connected to home.

Search up supports for international students – many tips sheets and articles about studying abroad are available online.[4]

She had taken her time selecting the university. Her mom came with her for on-site visits, and she had a feeling of "this is it" when she came to this campus. The first week seemed amazing, and she felt like she met a lot of people. But looking back, she didn't really get to know any of them. Making friends in university is much harder than most students think it's going to be.

Maybe you identify with this? Perhaps you long for all that was familiar and those who know you best. Homesickness is a combination of missing what was and not yet being connected to what is (or could be). As Nelly Spigner, an undergraduate student interviewed by *Time Magazine*, said, when you're going through stress, "it doesn't seem like anyone else is going through what you're going through."[5]

Let me assure you, it's not only normal to feel homesick, according to a BBC article by Tom Heyden, it's actually quite common.[6] Almost 70 percent of first-year students who move away from home to attend school feel homesick in the first term.[7] For about 5 percent, this homesickness morphs into a kind of sadness that interferes with academic performance, making dinner, and getting out of bed. Most of us experience homesickness as something that comes and goes in waves.[8] When you feel a surge of homesickness coming on, it's important to do a few things differently.

Being in a new environment with serious academic demands can be overwhelming, but October has other strains too. It's hard to make lasting friendships, and this is the time of year when high-school connections really shift. For example, many Grade 12 sweethearts attempt to stay together, but by Thanksgiving weekend they realize that the long-distance relationship isn't working. It's so common that it has its own slang name – the turkey dump. If you're managing a breakup while you're also facing midterms – you aren't alone.

Setting yourself up with some structure and support will help. Positive reinforcement (pleasant experiences that help you to do more positive behaviours) is the best kind of motivator for most of us. Positive reinforcement is when someone says hello to you when you're out and about on campus, when your professor hands you back a strong grade that reflects your hard work, and when you wake up feeling wonderful after a solid night's sleep (from knowing you're back on track). To get your behaviour moving in the right direction, you may want to talk with a parent, trusted friend, or a university counsellor. It's easier to get out of the isolation trap if you have support. Self-compassion is also required as you grow into your new-found freedom. You have more on your plate – certainly more homework – but you also have more choice and latitude to do what you want. Making the transition takes time, and change takes effort. Stick with it and get outside.

S Is for Sidetracked

University life is full of choices, some tiny, others massive – and we're all bound to get sidetracked from our goals now and then.

Sometimes getting sidetracked puts us on a damaging path, and it can be hard to get back on course. There's no need for anyone to be preachy about it; it's more about getting back on track than casting judgment.

Jenny was underage when she started university. When she reached legal age, she took up the bar life with gusto. She loved the sound of ice tinkling in her glass and craved the feeling she had on the dance floor. With a bit of so-called liquid courage, she found herself striking up conversations. For a while, she found she was less lonely, more active, and maybe even more focused when she was in her course lectures. But her shyness remained, and Jenny still felt awkward most of the time. She daydreamed about evenings out and was distracted by memories of feeling free.

Jenny knew she was off track when she started drinking away from the bar scene, when she found herself sipping vodka in the afternoon before class. Her poor choices were reinforced by the social ease they gave her and her freedom from self-monitoring. She drifted along in the direction of self-medication until she forgot why she was drinking. It just became something she did. She could no longer track what was happening in her classes. Irritability and foggy thinking made it hard to connect with the people she met, but she found them incredibly annoying anyway. Her sleep became erratic, she skipped assignments, and when it came to midterms, she crashed and burned.

Concerned, Jenny's roommate and parents initiated an intervention. If Jenny wanted to continue with university, something was going to have to change. There was a blow-up, and some tears, but Jenny decided that university was important to her. Jenny decided to stay in school but moved home for support. She took time off work and used some of that time to meet with a therapist to focus on social anxiety and interpersonal communication. When she felt more at ease with herself, she joined a women's hip-hop dance class and later joined the campus dance club. Real friendships developed there, and she found herself living and socializing without the aid of alcohol.

It's not unusual for students to drink or do drugs, and experimenting with the feeling of inebriation is not in itself a bad thing. However, according to the NCHA survey, 20 percent of students had experienced being "black-out drunk" in the past year, and 26 percent said they did something while drunk that they later regretted. About 5 percent of university students reported using alcohol or marijuana daily. Alcohol addiction and drug abuse are complicated experiences and hard to identify (let alone address) on your own. Jenny's story could have easily been about dependence on pot, over-the-counter pain medications, or "harder drugs," or gambling, gaming, or even video chatting with strangers. All of these activities have the potential to light up the pleasure centres of our brain and can cause cravings or addictions. Going on a binge is another form of being sidetracked that causes students to lose their academic focus. If you're sidetracked in these ways, please seek support.

QUICK TIP ⚡

Drinking for courage is actually a misnomer. According to a *Daily News* article by Annie Grace, alcohol is actually linked with increased anxiety. According to her sources, drinking alcohol can increase our heart rates and change the serotonin levels in our brains. This can increase our feelings of general anxiety and make panic attacks much more likely. She concludes that drinking for courage is a big mistake, and besides, most of us know that the drunken courageous person usually comes off as a self-centred ass.[9]

H Is for High Expectations

At one end of the continuum, you have the students who coast or get sidetracked; at the other end you have students who are under pressure to get straight A's, no matter what. Whether they have an internal drive or are responding to the high expectations of parents, those who tend towards perfectionism are inclined to crash. Rarely happy, often pressured, and high-strung, perfectionists tend to complicate tasks. They're more likely to procrastinate on starting projects either because they're distracted by perfecting other assignments or because they unconsciously want to give themselves a way to save face (if I had had more time, it would have been perfect). Through your university years, you'll likely learn how to temper your perfectionism and evolve into the realm of high achievers who know how to sustain their excellence over time.

Perfectionists	High Achievers
• Driven by fear	• Driven by enjoyment
• Focused on fear of failure	• Focused on pride of achievement
• Results are all that matter	
• Expectations are unrealistically high, setting them up to feel inadequate	• Learn from experience – the outcome is only one measure of success
• Can tolerate mistakes by others but cannot tolerate mistakes of their own	• Expectations are high but achievable with hard work, setting them up for success
• Have a hard time being critiqued or having their work criticized	• Can tolerate mistakes from themselves and others and see them as learning opportunities
• Tend to be rigid and feel devastated when things go wrong	• Criticism is welcomed if it helps them to improve
• Prone to procrastination; they put things off as a way to protect their ego ("It would have been perfect if I had had more time")	• Tend to be flexible and resilient
	• Less prone to procrastination and more excited about what's possible

Crash Pads and Getting Back on Track

If you hit a wall and crashed in October, it's likely for one of the reasons listed above. You've been coasting on your high-school smarts, reacting to things instead of taking a proactive approach, coping with isolation and that feeling of being alone, sidetracked by other situations, or trying to reach unrealistically high expectations. In response to these situations, I offer these crash-pad suggestions. The October crash is not actually the crisis it appears to be. Failing a midterm (or several) sucks, but it's what you do next that really counts. Let's soften the blow and get you up and moving again.

Do Not Quit.
October is not the right time to ditch a class or drop out of school. It's too early in the game. Since most of your marks will come in the last half of the semester (essays, projects, quizzes, and final exams), there will be plenty of time to reform your habits and recover academically. Sometimes we tell ourselves that dropping a course will leave more time for the other classes we're taking, but I think we know that's actually not true. If you're full-time, you want to keep that advantage. If you're part-time, then we want to keep you in class as much as we can. Besides, if you drop out now, you won't get any of your money back, so you might as well stay in the class and test out a few different approaches.

Form an Exit Plan, but Don't Use It Yet.
All universities specify a withdrawal deadline. This is the last date when you can drop out of a class without an academic penalty. The course will still appear on your transcript, but the grade assigned will be a "W" (standing for *withdrawal*). This W-grade won't count towards your overall grade point average, but it does show that you attempted the course and dropped out. Though you don't get any money back, it's much better to have a W than an F in a course, because an F counts as a zero in the calculation of your GPA. More on that later (or flip to Chapter 13 for details).

Withdrawing from a class can be an academically sound decision, but it does leave a mark on your transcript. If you have your eyes set on law or medical school, a W on your transcript might impact your admission. Even if your goal is not a professional degree, October is too early in the academic semester to make that withdrawal decision.

For now, all you need to know is the date of the withdrawal deadline. Find it in your university's calendar, and schedule it into your phone. Circle the day on your wall calendar and ask your parents to remind you of it. As the date approaches, you can decide whether to stay in the course, but for now you need to give it an honest try.

Reach Out to Your Instructors.
Let your professor, instructor, or TA know that things aren't going well, and see what they suggest. You can reach out through an email (just don't start it with "Hey"), but going in person is usually recommended. I understand that going to a professor's office hours can be intimidating, but the extra support you find there can be amazing. You might also consider connecting with a tutor (often free on campus), or see if there's a study support room you can access. At my university, the Math Lab is available to anyone with a math question (math major or not). You might find that there's a biology study centre or an open-studies hour where faculty, grad students, or staff are available for support. These spaces are terrific for "on-demand" help with specific questions. Your professors will have some good recommendations.

STUDENT STORY

I was struggling with a computer science project, and I couldn't find a tutor to help me with the coding. I asked the prof to introduce me to a stellar student from last year, and they actually offered to tutor me for free. It was good experience for their résumé, and talking through my program glitches helped me find the errors. Amazing.
– MOCHAMAD

Suck It Up and Get Back Out There.
This sounds harsh to say (and even to write), but it's true. The good part about crashing in October is that you still have plenty of time to recover. It serves as a wake-up call – a kick in the ass to take your studies more seriously with a focus on persistence, not perfection.

STUDENT TIP ⚑

I've heard it said that C's get degrees – and that may be true in some cases. At my university, though, I had to have a competitive average to make it into my program after a generalized first year. My advice? Look ahead and read the fine print about admission and graduation requirements, prerequisite classes, and grad school, if that's your destination.
– CHARLES

They say that after you've had a car accident the best thing you can do is get back behind the wheel as soon as possible. The same can be said of embarrassment or anxiety – they'll only go away if you challenge them. Many students stop going to class because they're feeling bad about skipping class, failing midterms, or both. I'm confident that your professor would want you to return to class. I'm also confident that many of your professors have seen students experience the October crash many times throughout their career. Many have also had first-hand experience failing midterms back in their own undergrad days (I certainly did). It's more normal than you realize.

To get back on track, you're going to need to set your emotions aside (for now), do a complete review of the facts, decide what to do, and then enact that plan. Here are the steps to take:

Calculate Your Win Ratio. To transform your poor midterm grade into a motivational force, grab your course outline to calculate what you need to do to win. If you want to get a pass in the course, what kinds of grades do you need to get through the rest of the term to pull that off? For example – if your midterm was worth 15 percent of your overall grade and you got 0 on it, can you still pass the course?

Absolutely.

In fact, you only need to get 70 percent on everything else to get 60 percent in the course overall, and that's with a 0 on that first midterm. If you wrote the exam, it's unlikely you got 0. Most fails are in the 40 percent range (in our example, that would be 6 points out of 15). With a 40 percent (fail) on the first midterm, worth 15 percent of the overall grade, you only need to get 65 percent on each of the remaining assignments or tests to get a 60 percent overall.

Check If Your Final Exam Is Cumulative. This is super important. If your final exam is NOT cumulative – that means that what you've covered (and failed to know) for the midterm will not be on the final exam. You can start now with a clean slate and begin to do things differently through to the end of the course. If the final exam is cumulative, it means that the things you covered on the midterm will also show up on the final exam. In this case, you absolutely have to catch up on what you've missed. No beach-holiday reading week for you.

Review Your Mistakes. Take your midterm exam into the learning centre (student learning services, academic support centre, whatever it's called in your university) and review your work with a learning strategist. These services will be free, and your session will be with a professional (or a senior peer). They'll help you with test-taking strategies, and you'll leave with fresh ideas about how to approach your next exam. Reviewing the exam with your course TA (teaching assistant) is also an excellent strategy. Though you might be intimidated at first, most professors are glad to talk content with their students. Go to the professor's office during their posted office hours and get some free, individualized advice.

Then Do Things Differently. Once you have the withdrawal deadline saved, know your odds of passing (which are likely very good), and have reviewed your exam with your prof or a learning strategist, you'll need to learn some new study habits and then use them. Now is not the time to slow down. It's time to rev up.

Ottavio Perri was a high-school teacher for fifteen years, and a vice-principal for another ten. His son Patrick Perri teaches computing at Mount Royal University. Patrick (and his dad) warns students about the October turn, saying that many students want to take a break at the sharpest part of the curve (the dark depths of October, or February). His father's advice? "Don't stop. If you do, you'll spin out. Instead, as you head out of that turn, that's the time to accelerate by applying yourself the most."

There are more turns ahead, and as you approach them, slow down to take stock of your priorities, but don't stop. Once you're focused on what's most important, hit the gas and accelerate into that turn. Experience will improve both your courage and your tactics. Take Mr. Perri's advice. Keep going.

Key Messages

☆ The October crash is a real thing. It happens to most first-year students, and it's mentally exhausting.

☆ Common reasons why students crash include:

> COASTING. Many smart students coast through high school or CEGEP without building solid study skills. Coasting in university doesn't work; sometimes these smart students have terrible midterm marks. Building great study strategies is the key.

> REACTIVE. Sometimes when things just aren't going well, we get overwhelmed, cranky, and upset at ourselves and those around us. Learn to be proactive and responsive.

> ALONE. Homesickness is a real thing, and it impacts our ability to sleep, concentrate, remember, and perform. Knowing you're not the only one who feels this way will help, and counselling support can be valuable.

> SIDETRACKED. There are many distractions in university, and some of them can knock us off course. Keeping substance use or other "risky behaviours" in check can help us meet our bigger goals.

> HIGH EXPECTATIONS. If we're taking it all too seriously, we may be too rigid or perfectionistic in our approach, which could lead to poor results. High achievers generally outperform perfectionists, but perfectionism can be hard to work through. Seek support from learning strategists, counsellors, and peer mentors to get back on track.

☆ Make an exit plan to withdraw – but don't use it yet. It's too early to drop a course or bow out of the term.

☆ Calculate your win ratio, and then get back out there. It's time to accelerate into the curve.

MAYBE I'M NOT SMART ENOUGH

Do I belong here?
Am I the only one who is struggling? Should they have let me in?
What are successful students doing that I can learn from?
How can I untwist negative thinking and improve my focus?

MAYBE I DON'T belong here or *I'm going to fake it 'til I make it* are common thoughts among first-year students. If the walls of my counselling office could talk, they would share a thousand stories that begin with the same doubts. "I'm not good enough." "I'm worried about sounding stupid." "Everybody is staring at me." Imposter syndrome is an actual thing. Wondering if you're smart enough is a common concern, and I know it feels real.

Right after the October crash, Benny came into my office feeling this way. With three assignments due in the next week and another set of tests on the horizon, he was overwhelmed with the workload. He was already behind in his readings and felt that everyone else was on top of things. He dismissed his past achievements as luck and assumed that he would be facing a failing mark on the test he wrote that morning. He was embarrassed by his performance and said he had skipped class to meet with me.

It's like watching a person leap over all of their skills and past accomplishments to crash into a pit of self-doubt and despair. He slumped into one of my soft counselling chairs and said he had never felt so out of place. He shared the typical kind of thinking that makes us feel all alone. He told me that everyone else in the class "knows what's going on." "They have it together."

Those assumptions served to reinforce his negative thinking, reflected in statements like "I'm the only one who doesn't get this. I don't belong here."

He concluded that he was not smart enough to make it in university, and he said that it was only a matter of time until his profs figured out that accepting him was a mistake.

I couldn't just tell Benny that his fears were normal and that these thinking traps were common – he wasn't in my office to receive platitudes – he needed to work through these feelings, explore the evidence, and consider new conclusions. Based on his grades through high school and the fact that he was accepted into a competitive program, I think it's fair to say that Benny "had the smarts" for university. But being smart isn't enough. What else are successful students doing that Benny could learn from?

Consider this. I was part of a study with two professors from my university's Economics program – Young Jung and Ambrose Leung.[1] Both of these men love to teach and, like me, they're interested in helping students succeed. They approached me to help them investigate whether smart students study harder. We looked at how students spend their leisure and study time and then compared patterns to grades.

The formulaic model we deduced is complicated, and as someone who never took macro- or microeconomics, I found it incredibly difficult to understand but also fascinating to look at. Here's one of the formulas we worked with:

$$\frac{dE}{dI} = \frac{\beta U_w(w_G G_I + w_I)}{U_L - \beta U_w(w_G G_L + w_K K_L)} > 0$$

What? Ha! Talk about not feeling smart enough!

Working with these two experts took a toll on my confidence – but we made it fun, we took things slowly, and we honoured our different ways of thinking. Put into regular words, the formula above describes the findings of our study: high-achieving students don't spend more time studying, but they do study more efficiently. They were more likely to spend their study time with friends and classmates. They combined social time with academics, which made the work more efficient (and likely more fun). Working with others allows us to practise, discuss, and teach others. This is important for learning because memory consolidation is best when we've had a chance to use the information we've newly acquired. The social aspect also means we're likely to take breaks while studying, which improves memory retention and stamina. "Smart" students don't study harder; they just study smarter – more efficiently and more socially. We called this *efficient effort,* and it's worth trying, for sure.

Self-Doubt Gets in the Way of Fun

Like most of us, when you're stressed you likely tend to minimize the positives and externalize them: *That was nothing* or *I was just lucky.* Then, to make things worse, you might maximize the negatives and internalize them: *There must be something really wrong with me. I've never been good at that.* Stress also makes the positives sound transient and the negatives feel more permanent. One is a moment in time; the other is just the way things are.

It's not just you, and it's not just Benny. We can all get caught in these kinds of traps. When we're stressed out, we become vulnerable to this kind of thinking. It's like some kind of stress monster. It lurks in the dark until it senses your vulnerability, then it lunges out and traps your thoughts, dragging them into a downward spiral, devouring your soul. Actually, maybe not your soul, but you know what I mean.

Starting first year is certainly stressful. The October crash is stressful. So are the first finals of your final year, the first days of work, or any time you have to go through something unfamiliar, important, or intimidating. It's normal to fall prey to these kinds of stress monsters, but we don't want to stay in their grip.

Let's break it down by looking at our worries with intention. One of my favourite intervention phrases is *Look it in the eye.* Once we know what we're dealing with, we can figure out a plan.

Evaluate the Evidence

What if you're like Benny, and you feel worried that you're not smart enough to be in university? Let's look at the facts first. Acceptance

THINKING TRAPS AND TIPS

It's common to get stuck in a pattern of negative thoughts, and anxiety can sometimes twist or distort our thinking into irrational channels. Drawing on Aaron Beck's cognitive behavioural therapy model,[2] Anxiety Canada (anxietycanada.com) outlines several common thinking traps:

- All-or-nothing thinking: finding it hard to think about possible outcomes that aren't really good or really bad.

- Worst-case thinking: getting stuck imagining the worst-case scenario, regardless of how unlikely that outcome might be.

- Overestimating: thinking that if it happened once, it will happen again, and it will be worse.

- Mind reading: assuming that people are thinking negatively about you without any concrete evidence to back up that conclusion.

- Exaggerating and internalizing the negative: not recognizing that some things are going well and only paying attention to the test marks you missed or the one thing that went wrong.

- Minimizing and externalizing the positive: dismissing good experiences as luck or dismissing compliments as people simply being nice.

To rescue yourself from a thinking trap, the first step is to acknowledge that it's happening. Listen for self-talk that includes the words always or never, and look for the patterns mentioned above.

To untwist your thinking, do the following:

- Use mindfulness to watch the thought come and go.

- Examine the evidence: Do the facts support your conclusion?

- Challenge yourself to "own" the positive (getting that A- wasn't about luck; it reflected my effort and organization).

- Challenge yourself to consider that next time could be better.

- What would I say to a friend who's thinking this way?

- Put it in its place: will this issue matter to you a year from now?

rates at most universities are not 100 percent, and it's not just random luck that you got in. You likely beat out other candidates who also wanted to be in your place.

If you aren't currently in university but want to be one day, then you get extra kudos for reading this book now. You're ahead of the game. The fact that you're thinking in advance about managing the transition into university shows that you're the kind of person who prepares, thinks ahead, and sets goals. Keep going!

If you did get into university, you must have had decent grades, you took the courses that were required for admission, and you may have demonstrated your talent (through audition or portfolio) to get through the door. To claim that you're not smart enough to be here doesn't hold weight. Colleges and universities have been doing this for a long time; they want to accept students who are likely to graduate and succeed – thus improving the reputation of the institution and providing an incentive for others to apply. Are you smart enough to be here? The proof is in your acceptance. Right?

Benny couldn't argue with that logic either.

School Success Isn't Really about Intelligence

Really – it's not. Success in postsecondary is mostly about attitudes and habits (aha!).

Consider this example. One of my long-time colleagues, Todd Nickle, is a biology professor at Mount Royal University known for having high expectations of his students. He is a sweetheart of a human being, but as a student, you'd likely find him intimidating and demanding. The intimidation subsides over time, but I don't think the demands do.

Todd wants his students to have a solid base for success. The stronger you are in your first-year foundational courses, the easier upper-level courses will be. He tells his students what skills and knowledge they need to acquire and exactly how to get there.

Todd tracked student grades and student attendance in his courses for several years, and then he invited me to be part of a formal study to look at how these variables connect.

Our findings?

Students who got A's generally did not skip class.

They weren't perfect – maybe they missed one or two lectures – but that's it. Every student who got an A attended nearly every class. Okay. A-students go to class. Great.

But wait, there's more!

Students who went to class all the time did not fail.

If you go to class – missing only one or maybe two through the term – you're going to pass the class. You'll need to do other work to earn an A, but you're pretty much guaranteed to pass the course just by attending. Okay, it's not exactly guaranteed; ideally, you're also doing some readings. And, of course, you need to be *in* class – mentally present, engaged, and listening to the prof. Not on your phone. And you need to hand in your assignments and show up for tests, but all of this will be easier if you regularly go to class.

I recognize that not every class is going to be identical to Todd's, but year after year this was the pattern in his classes.

So if you go, you'll pass. Study, review, and practise and you'll likely move up towards that A. Another way of looking at it is this:

Every student who failed Todd's class missed three or more classes.

Maybe you're thinking that students who start to fail also start to miss class because they're stressed or embarrassed. This is certainly what happened to Benny. He was missing class to sit in my office. He felt too embarrassed to face his peers and his prof. He was too worried about his classes to be in them.

This is understandable, but it's not helpful. If you tank an assignment or midterm, yes, it's hard to go back. It's embarrassing and stressful. Maybe you're pissed off at yourself or, more likely, at the teacher (sorry, Todd). Tired, embarrassed, confidence shot, maybe you're thinking, *If I'm going to fail anyway, why bother going to class?* "What do you want me to do?" you might ask.

I want you to get your ass back to class.

Put on a hoodie, pull on a ballcap. Creep in as the clock strikes the hour. Sit in the back, sit along the far wall. Don't talk to people if you don't want to. Do what you need to do to get there. But go.

So, in Benny's case, part of my intervention focused on getting him back to class. Even though no one does a roll call in university, it's important for him to be in the classroom and exposed to the material. We arranged to meet between classes, and I encouraged him to go back to class, even though he would be walking in late. Most university professors would rather have you arrive a few minutes late than miss a class altogether.

STUDENT TIP ⚑

Treat your class like a no-phone zone – don't even take it out during class; it will only distract you. You don't have to be here – you have choice. And you're paying to be here – it's important. So be here. Put the phone away. Shop later. Listen now. – ROSA

Following this session, Benny and I also talked about smarter studying and efficient effort. We talked about all the typical self-care things too – sleep, nutrition, laughter, and exercise – because the healthier we are, the better we function. When you feed yourself what you need on all levels – emotional, physical, social, intellectual, and spiritual – you'll feel better, you'll find your groove, and your studying will be more efficient.

Mull that over as you walk yourself to class.

FUN FACT

Online learning also relies on class attendance. If you find yourself in a distance-learning situation, attending those virtual lectures will improve your grades. Schedule your time so you can be fully present, and resist the urge to multi-task while class is on. Your performance in the course will be improved by taking notes while you listen and engaging with your prof and your peers through activities, chat boxes, and assignments.

Key Messages

☆ If you're questioning your ability to succeed in university, you're not alone. This kind of doubt seems to be part of the undergraduate process. It's a phase, and people can help you resolve it.

☆ When our stress is high, we tend to minimize the positives in our life and externalize them. (I was lucky. It was an easy thing. My roommate got me through it.)

☆ When our stress is high, we also tend to maximize the negatives and internalize them. (It's all my fault. This is awful. I can't believe I messed up.)

☆ Confront those thinking traps by looking them in the eye. Evaluate the evidence and act accordingly.

☆ School success isn't really about intelligence. It's about effort. It's about hard work. Studies show that smart students are great at efficient effort – working smarter, not harder.

☆ Part of efficient effort is going to class.

☆ The relationship between class attendance and academic success is clear. Students who go to every class rarely fail, and students who get A's go to nearly all of their classes.

☆ Challenge yourself to put your phone away during classes and aim to be fully present. The more you engage with the class, the more information you'll retain. This efficient effort will show in your grades.

TIME MACHINES
AND HOW TO USE THEM

How can I fit this all in when there aren't enough hours in the day?
Do I have to do the readings?
How do I figure out what will be on the exam?

ONE OF THE biggest complaints students have is not having enough time. It adds to their feeling of not being smart enough or not having a grip on life. Then the downward spiral happens. You cut corners, skip readings, miss deadlines, or do a half-assed job just to get the paper in. Then you feel awful because you didn't do what you wanted to do, which leads to feelings of shame about the other things you're doing or not doing. Down, down, down into that dark hole.

This happened to Em. As a varsity basketball player, she was up at the crack of dawn (and often before), hitting the gym hard with her teammates by 6:00 a.m. There was cardio training, weight lifting, and interval circuits to be done, and, of course, hours of game time each week too. She had to keep up a C average to stay on the team but, honestly, it was hard to focus on academics between training, home games, and being on the road. The hole Em fell into felt like total despair. Basketball was her only love, yet she needed to keep up her school work to stay with the team. She didn't feel she could do it. Em had always thought she was a bit of a dumb jock, not book-smart. On the court, she felt confident, but away from the game, she got stressed. She always felt like she needed more time to get things done.

Struggling to find your way academically doesn't mean you're not smart enough, but it does mean you have to do something different with your attitude and effort if you want to get a different kind of grade. As Young Jung, Ambrose Leong, and I found, smart students study efficiently. Efficient students also use multiple strategies to manage their time.

Calculate Your Class Hours and Study Time

There comes a time when it's going to feel like there just aren't enough hours in the day to get the work done. In addition to going to class, you'll have deadlines to manage and tests to study for. You'll have chapters to read, articles to find, papers to draft, groups to meet with, and notes to review. On top of the workload, you'll want to also fit in time with friends, earn some money at work, volunteer somewhere, talk with your family, and sleep. Time management is one of those life skills that university is going to demand you master.

When it feels like the walls are starting to close in on you, believe it or not, it's time to do some math. Crunching these kinds of numbers will relieve a lot of your stress. Let's take it in steps:

1. Start with counting up the hours you have in class (include labs, seminars, and so on). A full-time student likely has at least 15 hours of lecture time, and maybe another 3 hours of labs or tutorials. Add up your hours and start a running total.

2. Next, add in your study time. My friends in student-learning services generally say that we need 3 hours of studying for each hour of class. So, if you're taking 15 hours of class (at my university, that means 5 classes at 3 hours each), then you need to budget in 45 hours of studying.

When Alyssa heard this, she was blown away. Her university schedule alone required more than 60 hours a week of effort. No wonder she was having a hard time fitting other things in. This also helped her to understand why the transition from high school felt so hard. Alyssa basically doubled her school load when she entered university. Looking back on her October crash, she admitted that this math made sense.

The week gets busier though as we add in other commitments.

3. Next, add 8 hours of sleep per day and an hour of transition time on each end – that is, an hour to wake yourself up and an hour to wind down. That's 70 hours a week. Add more if you love to sleep. Some people crave 10 hours a night, which is terrific – but 12 is likely too much. Try not to go below 7 hours a night – your brain is still developing, and this time in life is taxing on our system. You're in a high-learning phase, and your body needs to sleep to make sense of it all.

Added together, Alyssa saw that she was using 70 hours of her week for sleep, and another 63 hours for classes, her lab, and studying. The week only has 168 hours in it, so she was left with just 35 hours of "spare time." Time to use for other things like employment, working out, commuting, eating, bathing, and taking breaks to socialize or zone out. Just based on this math alone, she was going to need to become more efficient in order to fit everything in.

Efficiency Hacks – Ways to Find More Time

Remember the study by my colleagues Jung and Leung about smart students studying more efficiently? Let's talk about how to make that happen.

Take Notes

In university, you need to take notes during lectures. It's proven that we remember better when we write things down with an actual pen on an actual piece of paper (compared to typing things out or just listening). The act of writing is better than the act of typing. Muscle memory is a real thing, and when you write, you're engaging more of your mental capacity and sparking several kinds of memory:

- *Auditory memory:* what you're hearing.
- *Visual memory:* what you see or the words or diagrams you put down on the page.
- *Muscle or kinesthetic memory:* what your body remembers of the experience of writing (writing is more complex than typing, which adds richness to our memory).

- *Semantic memory*: your understanding of what the words, ideas, and concepts mean.

Together, these types of memory form an episodic memory of the class, and the richer this experience is, the more of a memory you'll have of that episode of your life. When you're trying to recall something during an exam – you'll have visual, auditory, and kinesthetic cues to link to the meaning of the material.

WHY TAKE NOTES?

- Focuses you on the lecture, not your phone
- Improves memory and recollection of facts and figures
- Shows gaps in understanding
- Helps to synthesize knowledge and consolidate learning
- It's a creative outlet, especially when colour, sketches, mind mapping, or images are blended in
- Provides physical cues (such as the above) to draw on when writing an exam – you're more likely to give correct answers if you can remember writing them down in class
- Makes studying more efficient if you've listened with the intention of understanding
- Supports exam success by helping you recognize repetition (if a professor says a fact more than once, it's likely going to show up on an exam)
- Can be a great way to meet people ("Did you get that part down?," "Can I see how you captured that?," "Wanna get together after class and compare notes?")

Colour coding your notes is not required but, for many, it keeps it fun and lighthearted and helps them stay focused on the task. It also adds dimension to the episode, which might make it easier to remember later.

A FEW MORE NOTES ABOUT NOTES

Creating good notes from a university lecture requires some serious skill. I like the way the College Info Geek's blog post, "How to Take Better Notes: The 6 Best Note-Taking Systems," likens university classes to the Big Boss of the video game world.[1] Whatever weapons you used to slay your high-school classes will be inadequate for university life. You're going to need to level up.

There are many strategies for note taking. Try them out.

- Make an outline from the textbook and then fill it in during the lecture.

- Take notes following the lecture and then make brief notes later based on those lecture notes.

- Keep consolidating your notes down until you have a one-sheet summary page or a set of flash cards.

- For a next-level approach, make your notes into a practice test. Include short-answer questions, fill in the blanks, and "define this term" questions. Do the test without your books and under a time limit.

Other cues that students find helpful include having a particular book or binder for each class, sitting in the same seat, or using symbols to anchor their attention to important things. Carlos puts a star beside things he thinks will be on the exam, and he highlights the things he doesn't quite understand – to look them up later.

There are experts on your campus who can give you more tips. Recall that Donnie had two meetings with a learning strategist where he learned some tips for taking great notes. He also joined a peer-study group where he was mentored by upper-year students who gave him tips on what profs want and don't want:

- If a piece of information is presented in class and is also in the textbook, then it will likely show up on the exam.

- If a piece of information is not in the textbook but is mentioned in class, then it will likely be on the exam.

- Profs like to put their own spin on the material, and they like to test you about it too.

Taking notes will help you to see these overlaps and distinctions. I'm confident that these kinds of services are available at your school and most likely free. Go and find them.

Follow the Five-and-Dime Rule

I've been using the phrase *five and dime* for years, but I don't mean it as an ode to the dollar-store equivalents of the 1920s. I mean that if you take five minutes in one place and ten minutes in another, your return on that studying investment will be astounding. The five-and-dime technique makes your studying more efficient, and because it's so strong, I think it's a rule all students should follow.

Here's how it works:

You know those great notes you just took in your lecture? Reviewing them will help solidify your memory of that class, and it's best to do that review right away. So, if you can, stay for ten minutes after class and reread your notes. Read them all the way through. Do this within an hour of the lecture if you can.

- Correct your spelling mistakes on key terms.

- Make sure everything is legible.

- Underline what seems most important.

- Highlight what you don't understand.

- Put a check beside what you have seen in the textbook. (Remember: if something appears in the lecture and the text, it is a strong candidate for an exam question.)

That ten minutes of review is the dime. Once you have read through the notes, put them away and head on to what is next on your schedule. Done. The five comes just before you have the next lecture in that class. Before the lecture starts, go in and spend five minutes reviewing the notes you took last class. This review will activate your memory, getting your brain ready to integrate new information. If you're confused about something in your notes, or if it looks like your information is incomplete, ask the professor to explain that part again.

QUESTIONS FOR PROFESSORS

If you have a question for your professor, it is completely okay to ask. If you email your professor, that email should come from your university account and should be more formal than what you would send to a friend. Asking questions face-to-face is also great. University professors will post weekly office hours when they will be available to speak with students. You can also ask questions before the lecture or at the end of class. For communication tips, consider these resources from the University of Toronto and the University of Waterloo:

- https://studentlife.utoronto.ca/task/talk-to-your-professors/

- https://uwaterloo.ca/writing-and-communication-centre/blog/post/importance-asking-your-professor

Combined with excellent note-taking skills, using five minutes before class and then ten minutes after each and every class to review your notes will cut your study time down by at least a third. For Alyssa, that could result in a savings of 15 hours every week. That's 15 hours she'll have back in her schedule to work, socialize, or slow down and relax. If you follow the five-and-dime rule, of course, you'll still have some horribly hard school weeks that will eat up those extra hours, but most weeks you'll have the ability to be on top of your workload.

Bonus outcomes, when it comes time to study for an exam, are that:

- Your notes will already be in great shape. They have been reviewed and corrected through the five-and-dime rule.

- Your memory will be in great shape – you've already read each of your lecture notes at least three times (once when you wrote them, and twice through the five-and-dime process).

- As a result, it will take you less time to study for any exam based on these notes.

STUDENT TIP 📌

CAUTION: If you're nice enough to share your notes with your buddy who missed class, text them photos of your work or walk together to the photocopier. If you lend your only copy out, you may never see it again. – JOE

Do the Least Preferred Thing First

If it's that journal entry you're avoiding, get it done first and out of the way. If you're dreading that email or really don't want to go get those articles from the library, then that's what you should start with. If you've got a sick feeling about a particular task, then getting it done will make you feel relief.

If you postpone the pain of doing something, you'll be stuck with the pain of thinking about it. That dread will weigh on you through the day and will interfere with your efficiency. Getting the least preferred thing out of the way first will give you space to feel better and get things done.

Don't Multi-task, Single-Task

Multi-tasking was once promoted as a way to save time, but we now know that most of us are terrible at doing two things simultaneously. What we're really doing when we're multi-tasking is switching between two tasks. This kind of attention-switching actually causes stress and reduces efficiency. We do better when we stick to one thing (watching a video, reading a chapter, having a conversation). Retraining your attention to stay on one thing for more than twenty minutes might take some time, but you can do it.

STUDENT TIP 📌

Study in a place that suits your style. Social buzz? Go to the café. Need quiet? Headphones, third-floor library by the window. – DONNIE

Set False Deadlines

Mikael started setting false deadlines in his second semester, and he hopes you'll start doing it right away. With one term under his belt, he vowed to stay more on top of his workload. During the first week of the new semester, he got all of his course outlines and began to figure out his plan. Two classes

STUDENT TIP
I eventually learned that multi-tasking in class is just a waste of time. If I'm shopping or surfing, then I'm not really listening, and if I miss stuff in class, it'll take me ten times longer to find it and learn it on my own. – MILES

had big endings: Aviation History and Air Law had a research essay worth 40 percent (due April 4), and Advanced Aviation Meteorology had a final assignment worth 35 percent (due April 5). Altogether, he was taking five classes with seven assignments, five tests, three presentations, four papers, a mega-essay, a mega-assignment, and three group projects (not to mention final exams).

With the chaos of last term fresh in his mind, Mikael made himself a semester plan. He bought one of those large, reusable wall calendars, the kind that shows four months at a glance, and began to plot out deadlines. The hot spots were clear. Time would be pinched in February, just before reading break, but it was really the first three weeks of March that were loaded. Then, curiously, there was a bit of a breather (a full week with no deadlines) before those term papers came due and final exams arrived. Knowing what he knows now – Mikael resisted the temptation to think that the semester looked light through February. Clearly, he would need that time to prepare for March Madness. Thinking strategically, Mikael decided he had to put his weeks in January to work for him. This is how he approached it:

1. Tackle small assignments first. He decided to get ahead on his Aviation Foundations course by drafting all six "reflection" papers by mid-January (instead of leaving them peppered throughout the semester). He handed three of them in and impressed his teacher. He decided to hand in the other three closer to Reading Week.

2. Find a group or group members eager to get things done. Mikael found group members who were interested in getting projects done early. This was a big relief and opened up a lot of time. They plotted out several meetings knowing their schedules would fill up fast.

3. Break big things into small chunks. Mikael broke his large essays, especially those that were worth 30 percent or more of his final grade, into smaller pieces. He created deadlines for picking a topic and library research and aimed to have at least three good sources for each paper before the reading break. He set dates for when he needed to have his "messy first drafts" done and felt that once these deadlines were in place the term looked doable.

4. Make realistic plans for Reading Week. Michael hoped to go away during Reading Week, but when he looked at his new schedule, he decided to schedule a four-day vacation (skiing with three close friends) instead. He'd leave just before Reading Week to hit the books steadily on the Tuesday of the break. The week after Reading Week would be a disaster if he didn't focus.

5. Schedule a reward to look forward to. Mikael's birthday (April 3) fell at quite possibly the worst time in the term. He decided that if he was going to have a decent birthday bash, he'd have to have everything done. Feedback from his friends reminded him that everyone was in the same boat. He decided to do a family brunch on his birthday and to "celebrate proper" on April 9, once classes were over. Wicked.

Stress and Perception

As Mikael's example shows, "smarter" learning is linked to how you approach the task in front of you. Are you scared of it or willing to take it on? Is it a threat? Or is it a challenge?

Most of the stress you feel in school is caused by how you're thinking about the situation, how you're looking at it. It's not about the situation itself.

Skeptical? Let's look at a few examples.

Joe has a psychology midterm tomorrow morning, and he's ready for it. He's been studying for two weeks (not straight, but consistently). He's been to every lecture, and most of the readings are done. There was one chapter, though, that he didn't really get to. He scanned it, and he read the summary, but neither is the same as a good review. Joe made up flash cards and used them on the bus ride to and from campus. He also made up two practice tests for himself. When he did them, he sat in an empty classroom and gave himself an hour – just like the real thing. Joe brought those mock tests to his prof to get some feedback, and he feels he's asking the right questions. He's using the midterm as a way to gauge whether he's on the right track with this class. He thinks he's getting it, and he's ready to see if he's right. Joe has stress, yes, but it's the kind that is keeping him focused and motivated. It's more excitement than worry.

Funnily enough, Rosa is taking the same psychology class as an elective for her nursing degree. It's not a priority for her, and it's totally different from what she's used to. She has a major exam for her anatomy class at the end of the week, and that's been taking up most of her study time. She went to the psych lecture the day before the exam and was overwhelmed by the review.

She realized she'd been neglecting the class and was going to be in trouble tomorrow. She hadn't even looked at one chapter yet. She had detailed notes on the others, which she's read over, but she wasn't sure how to study. Rosa is a perfectionist and takes exams seriously, but this one feels different because it's not in her field. She has booked five hours to sleep tonight, but she knows the worry will keep her up. Rosa doesn't feel confident, and the stress is making her nervous and scared.

Same class, same midterm, but different reactions. Joe and Rosa are facing the same situation, but their perceptions are different. They also have different kinds of resources: Joe has study strategies that are more tailored to this kind of exam while Rosa feels out of her element. Rosa has been neglecting this class in favour of her core courses, while this course is core for Joe. He's been keeping up, and he's ready for tomorrow.

STRESS = (SITUATION + PERCEPTION) – RESOURCES

Situations alone don't cause our stress – our interpretations of them affect the stress we feel. There are, of course, situations that are objectively stressful and would be experienced as stressful by most people.

For example, in 2013, when my city suffered a massive flood, many of its one million residents found the situation stressful. For some, it was emotionally devastating. Curiously, others found it stressful but manageable. These citizens found a way to cope with the stress, even in the face of significant loss. Somehow, even though they personally suffered tangible losses and the devastation of their homes, they were not emotionally devastated. Something about their interpretation of the situation provided them with an emotional buffer that lessened their stress levels. This is the power of resiliency and stress management.

Here's another example about something more common – cooking. Rosa loves to cook. It relaxes her, and she loves how it feels to feed her family and friends. It's challenging, sure, and sometimes things don't work out, but Rosa has confidence that she can manage the challenge. She can succeed by going slowly, checking the recipe, taste testing, and redoing if things go wrong. She also feels safe testing out new dishes on those who love her. Some of her mistakes have been hilarious and make for the best stories.

Joe, on the other hand, hates cooking. He finds it tedious, he doesn't do well with following recipes, and he doesn't have a flair for the corrective creativity that many recipes demand. Joe cooks, but only as required. He understands that making your own food is practical and saves money, but it's something he feels he has to do rather than something he wants to do. He avoids cooking for others because getting things wrong is embarrassing.

His mom still talks about the time he tried to cook a turkey and delayed their family dinner by 4 hours. Joe likes to think of it as an example of how stress can get in the way of thinking. The recommended 2 hours and 45 minutes was skilfully converted into 165 minutes. And the 165 was less skilfully converted into degrees instead of minutes. And, yes, there was the issue of the bird still being a bit frozen solid at the beginning of it all, but isn't it the thought that counts?

His mother likes to link this story to the time when he was three and he forgot to turn off the water in the bath, or the time when he was ten and insisted that he knew how the weed whacker worked. He's always the one person left not laughing.

For one person, cooking is stressful; for the other, it's not. Cooking, the event, is not the cause of the stress. There's something more going on. It's about the person's experience of the event. How they think about it and how they feel about it determines how much stress they experience.

It's the same way with exams.

Rosa finds exams quite stressful while Joe does not.

You may find an exam threatening or upsetting, or you may find it challenging or stimulating, as an opportunity to really see what you know. Understanding that your perceptions of an experience play a major role in the stress you feel provides a whole array of possible intervention strategies because instead of focusing on the situation (which often isn't going to change), you focus on your attitude and resources – things you absolutely can change.

FUN FACT

College students at Oxford were tested on attention and thinking speed then fed a five-day high-fat, low-carb diet heavy on meat, eggs, cheese, and cream. When tested again, their attention and speed performance declined. The students who ate a balanced diet that included fruit and vegetables held steady.[2]

Effort over Intelligence

Rosa would say that effort over intelligence has been key for her. In many ways, she doesn't feel like the sharpest tool in the drawer, but she sure does work hard. For her, putting in the time has made a difference. She reads things over several times and makes summary notes on her notes.

Joe makes flash cards and practice exams, which help him organize his thinking.

Carlos likes to talk through things with his peers and listen to debates (although he'd rather not participate in one).

Finding what works best for you will take some experimentation, but for most students, it's more about how you put the time in, rather than the intelligence you have. Smarts will get you started, sure, but it's effort that will make you succeed – regardless of your base intelligence.

In our study of student success and retention, we found that having a work ethic – how much you study, how often you go to class, and how good you are with deadlines – has more of an impact on grade-point averages and graduation than high-school English or Math marks.[3]

It's more about effort than intelligence. And to get back to that original mega-formula for success – it's efficient effort that we're talking about here. Working to your strengths, in your own stride, and based on what you want to do. Work smarter, not harder, and try to enjoy the process.

STUDENT TIP 📌

Play to your strengths. If you're visual, make cue cards; if you're conversational, join a study group. If you love watching videos, then find ones that match what your lectures are about. If you like to draw things out, the learning strategists told me about a mind-mapping strategy. Work to who you are rather than what you think you should be. – PHILLIP

Key Messages

☆ When we feel we're running out of time, we start to rush. Corners are cut and deadlines are missed. Learning to slow down is hard.

☆ It's time to do a time analysis. How many hours do you have, and how much study time do you need?

☆ Budget three hours of study time for each hour of class – EACH WEEK.

☆ Full-time university study is the equivalent of having a sixty-hour work week.

☆ Note taking in class will improve your memory.

☆ Join a peer group to study and compare notes. The most salient concepts covered in class will become obvious.

☆ Follow the five-and-dime rule consistently. Review your notes for ten minutes after every class and again for five minutes before class and you'll cut your study time by at least a third.

☆ Clear mental space by doing the least preferred thing first.

☆ Building in false deadlines can help with motivation. Using a semester-at-a-glance calendar can help you organize your priorities and build momentum.

☆ A huge portion of the stress we feel is caused by perception. We can apply this to exams by seeing them more as a challenge than a threat.

☆ Remember, your success has more to do with efficient effort than with raw intelligence. Organize your time and get ready to do the work.

MESSED UP
ABOUT MAJORS

What am I doing? How do I choose a major?
What if I'm in the wrong program and waste my time and money?
How do I make the right choice?

IT'S NOW A FEW months in, and you're not really sure about the program you're taking. Maybe you feel grateful for the acceptance you received, or perhaps you got five acceptance emails and rolled with the one that felt best or checked off the most boxes. Maybe you followed your parents' direction or went along with what your friends were doing.

Regardless of how you got here – you're here.

If you're uncertain about being in school right now or not sure if this particular program is where you want to be for the rest of your life, that's okay. In fact, it's pretty normal. Studies say that 70 percent of first-year students don't feel sure about their program choice. Nursing students wonder if social work would have been better, marketing students wonder about public relations, and engineering students wonder where the next party is…just kidding…sort of. Feeling unsure about where you are and what you're doing is not uncommon – it's what you do with that feeling that determines your success.

Before we change your uncertainty, let's try to understand it.

Uncertainty Is Normal
Let's start by acknowledging that uncertainty about your major is normal. Research reveals that most students, at some point, feel stressed about their eventual career choice – hence, changing majors is a common practice. In a study published by the National

Center for Educational Statistics in the United States, about 75 percent of students in four-year programs changed their major, and almost 10 percent changed their major *twice*. Those in STEM programs (science, technology, engineering, and math) were the most likely to abandon their original choice and take on a new major.[1]

Although uncertainty is common, it's not common knowledge that it is, leaving many students to suffer through it in isolation. It can feel like you're the only one who's questioning your program, and that's what makes uncertainty detrimental to your success. I've led three studies that tracked groups of students from their first weeks on campus through to graduation.[2] We found that for students in degree programs, feeling unsure about their major was the *number one* reason for dropping out of university. Not grades. Not finances. The main reason students drop out is uncertainty. In our follow-up interviews, students told us that they felt like they were alone in their uncertainty, like something was wrong with them and *only* them. They didn't realize that many students felt the same way.

Common Reasons for Uncertainty

The opening line of Leo Tolstoy's *Anna Karenina* is "Happy families are all alike; every unhappy family is unhappy in its own way." This rings true for the beginning of your undergraduate journey as well. It seems that everyone who feels great about their program feels that way for the same reason (it's a good fit), but everyone who is unhappy or uncertain about their choice has a personal reason for feeling that way. We can group these reasons into three general categories: uninterested, hesitant, and feeling overwhelmed.

Uninterested (Reality Didn't Meet Expectations)

After Joe decided he wanted to become a psychologist, he was excited to get on with it. He had found his calling. He wanted to become a therapist, to help individuals work through stuff and feel better about themselves and about life. What he didn't know as he walked into his first year was that psychology is a behavioural science that involves math, statistics, research, and theory. The first-year psych class was brutal – a lot of memorization and regur-gitation. He thought he would be working with clients but, instead, he ended up working with textbooks… and a pigeon (true story). To demonstrate his understanding of behavioural conditioning, Joe had to teach his pigeon (Bert) that pecking a red dot would deliver food. Then he had to test a series of reward schedules and measure how often Bert pecked that dot. It was as far away from talking with people as you could get. When Joe went to buy his second-term texts at the bookstore, he found himself casting covetous glances at the social work group-therapy books. He was envious and uncertain. Had he made the wrong choice?

Alyssa was in a totally different program but having similar doubts. As a marketing student, she found that most classes focused on persuasion, brand development, and trends, but she had a passion for organizing experiences and complex situations. She didn't want to advertise the event; she wanted to run it. When she met Mary in the Tim Horton's line, her mind was blown. Mary was studying public relations, and Alyssa felt her excitement rise as Mary described her classes. Alyssa had never even heard of PR, but media relations, event organization, and strategic communication planning felt more in line with what she wanted to be doing. Alyssa wanted to quit marketing and reinvent herself as a PR student immediately.

In my counselling practice, I've heard thousands of similar stories. This kind of uncertainty boils down to "this isn't what I thought it would be." Experience is an excellent informant. You don't know what something is really like until you try it. Trying to stay engaged when you aren't interested is draining. It's hard to stay motivated and engaged with classes or a program you're not loving. Something has to change.

Hesitant (Wondering If It's Worth the Effort)
The price of university is not paid in dollars alone. Going to school means giving up time you could be spending with friends or family. It means giving up on jobs and money earned. It also means

WHAT EMPLOYERS REALLY WANT

Most students worry too much about "the job" at the end of their degree. According to the Career Outlook report written by Domingo Angeles and Brian Roberts, trends show that most graduates end up working in jobs that aren't directly connected to their major.[3] In many cases, employers are looking for critical-thinking skills and communication expertise (hallmarks of all liberal arts degrees) rather than technical skills or even content expertise. These soft skills are essential to career success and will be embedded in any university program you take. In many ways, the best thing about university is that it teaches you how to learn, how to manage yourself, and how to succeed in the face of challenges.

spending less time doing stuff that you really love, like skiing, yoga, running, travelling – or whatever's your jam. An economist would call these *opportunity costs,* the things you give up to take advantage of an opportunity.[4] Through university, students also routinely feel overwhelmed and struggle with the stress of getting things done. And, yes, you're paying for this opportunity, right? Even if it's not your cash, it's your time and effort.

When you're not feeling confident that your investment will pay off, you may find yourself pausing to reassess the program you're in. You may feel hesitant about going forward. With all that you have to give up to go to school, will it be worth it in the end?

Sure, your critical thinking skills and writing will improve, and you'll manage your time better, but will you get a job?

I recently had a conversation about this with Rosie, a nursing student. Rosie is also a skier, a waitress, and someone who loves to travel. She always wanted to go into nursing – she was sure that it was the right choice for her – but after some brutal experiences at her first clinical placement and experiencing unrelenting high expectations that banged against her perfectionism, she questioned whether it was worth it. For Rosie, the first term was full of tears and doubt. Not self-doubt (she knows she's smart and capable of finishing the degree) – it's more a question of "success at what cost?," since no one can predict the future or guarantee employment.

Overwhelmed (Feeling Lost and Confused)

University is meant to open your mind to a multitude of possibilities. Minors, specializations, and electives will expose you to different disciplines and ways of thinking. You'll meet people from all over the world, and you'll encounter an array of viewpoints and perspectives. There will likely be times when this messes you up, when you feel overwhelmed and wonder if you've taken on too much.

This happened with Carlos. Like many students who come to university from a large high school, Carlos liked flying under the radar. A conscientious student, he did the work but didn't participate much in class. Following advice from his father and uncles, he majored in political science and came to university feeling at ease with his decision. But it didn't take long for Carlos to start feeling uncertain about his choice. One of his political science courses was divided into sections of about twenty students, and Carlos couldn't hide from daily debates and discussions on assigned readings. Students were called on to express their opinions and defend their positions. He began to reassess his beliefs as he became more aware of his biases, privileges, and limited exposure to dissenting opinions. This upheaval was positive, but Carlos said it also "messed with his head." His relaxed, easy-going attitude was replaced with apprehension. He wasn't sure if political science was still the right fit for him, but what choice did he have? No one else seemed to be caught in this turmoil.

QUICK TIP ⚡

If you're uninterested, hesitant, or feeling overwhelmed about parts of your life beyond school; if you've had more trouble sleeping or eating than normal; or if you feel sadder or more irritable than is normal for you – then more support is needed.

Go and speak with your university's student counselling team, or meet with a physician to talk about mental health. If you're experiencing depression, support will help you to get back on track with yourself and your studies.

It looked like everyone else was invested in the discussion, that he was the only one struggling to find his footing. Uncertain of how to proceed, he began to withdraw. It was harder to get things done, and getting to class felt like a struggle. Carlos began to think that maybe he wasn't ready for university after all.

The Upside of Uncertainty

Joe, Rosie, and Carlos were all uncertain about their majors, just like thousands of other undergraduates every year. If uncertainty is so common, perhaps it serves some kind of positive purpose? It does.

Who you are at the end of university will be very different from who you were at the end of high school, and uncertainty is the key antagonist in this transformation. You'll likely go from thinking you know it all to realizing you don't, likely never will, and don't have to.

If you feel uninterested, it could be because you're aware of new possibilities and can see beyond your first choice. If you're feeling hesitant, let that motivate you to investigate your choices and open yourself up to new ideas. Feeling overwhelmed indicates that you're being stretched in new directions, but it's also a sign of growth. Uncertainty can come up because you've changed or because your information has changed. Maybe your assumptions have been challenged, or maybe you're just open to new possibilities. In any case, you want to listen to that.

When you allow uncertainty to guide you, you still make progress, just not in a linear way. You'll learn more about what you do love by being exposed to what you don't. Negative interactions or unfulfilling experiences help shed light on our passions, values, interests, and preferences. If you find yourself in the wrong program, you're going to learn a lot about what you prefer to be doing. You're also going to learn a dozen transferable skills that will aid you in your career, including time management, self-motivation, attention management, grit, perseverance, self-awareness, critical thinking, analytical skills, and decision-making skills. Chalk it up to learning experiences. Remember, you're getting to know yourself, not just your program. Learning what you don't like is part of that process.

If you're facing uncertainty and you know in your heart, gut, or core that you're in the wrong program – then you'll grow a lot by switching over to the right one. You may be able to transfer courses without losing ground towards graduation, or you may need to repeat first year in that new program. Even if you lose a bit of time, have to make new friends, or need extra prerequisites – you'll be ahead of the game by doing what interests you. Ten years from now, it won't matter much if you had to take more time to finish an undergrad degree that you adored doing.

I wish more professors and parents would warn students that being unsure about your program is common, because even though Carlos felt like he was off track, he wasn't.

Feeling uncertain is more than normal, it's desirable. Carlos was totally engaged in his political science class – we know this because he was affected by it. He was thrown off by what he was hearing and reading. He was struggling to integrate these new ideas into what he had experienced in life so far. Although he felt alone in this, he wasn't. Other students in the class were almost certainly feeling challenged and overwhelmed. This is what makes university life-changing – it stretches you to think, reassess, and evolve.

Carlos talked with his professor during her office hours and told her about his stress. She encouraged him to do his term paper on the topic of opinion formation and to investigate how informed debate impacts the democratic process. This deep dive gave Carlos some insight into his own thoughts but also helped him understand the experience of being undecided and the importance of real news and informed discussion. He got a little more comfortable with his discomfort and found ways to be present in class even if he didn't have a clear opinion to share. He still wasn't sure that political science was right for him, but at least he found a way to not suffer through the courses he was in.

Don't Let Uncertainty Drive You Out of School

Feeling unsure is normal. Most first-year students spend part of the December break wondering if they've made the right choice, and 30 percent will change their major. Other shifts are common too. Many students change up their work hours, their attitudes, and their approach to studying. Uncertainty is not a problem, but running away from it, or letting it sit, unaddressed, can be. Give yourself some time to work it out, and don't let uncertainty lead you to dropping out. Although you may worry about it, keeping up with your current classes is probably not a waste of time or money. The courses you have now might count as electives in other degree programs, or these credits might transfer straight over as required courses (many degrees require a Math or English course, for example). Uncertainty will mess with your motivation, but I encourage you to keep going, at least until you can do a deeper dive and explore the meaning behind your discontent (see Chapter 15). The momentum you build up in first semester is something you don't want to lose.

Set a date in a week or two to re-evaluate your situation (put a flag in your calendar with an electronic reminder). Check into the application deadlines for various alternative programs, and book in to see an academic advisor a few weeks before that date hits. They can provide guidance about your options and walk you through the costs and benefits of switching majors. Advising is free and guaranteed to be time well spent.

Key Messages

☆ Uncertainty about your career or choice of major is common. Many first-year students, about a third, switch programs. If you're thinking of switching, you aren't alone.

☆ Common reasons for uncertainty include disinterest or unfulfilled expectations; hesitation as we wonder if it's worth the effort; and feeling overwhelmed by the volume of work required.

☆ There's an upside to uncertainty – it's a great teacher. Explore it and allow uncertainty to lead you in new directions. It could be the path to discovery.

☆ Set a date in the near future when you can reflect on your options for careers and majors.

☆ Consider how adding a minor to your career path could enhance your educational experience.

☆ Look for practical ways to exercise the new knowledge and skills you're learning. Practical work experience is also a great teacher and will bring clarity to your process.

☆ Seek support from your academic advisor, counselling team, and career-services staff. There are many professionals available to assist you.

10

THE SH*T HAS
HIT THE FAN

How can I stop myself from freaking out?
How can I get over a mistake and move on?
If I'm feeling desperate, where can I get help?

"THIS SHOULD BE pretty routine," says Avani, an aviation student, to Rita, her co-pilot.

"I don't know...The professor told us to prepare for the unexpected."

They're piloting a Cessna single-engine, four-seat aircraft, and today's task will require them to fly to an airport about 150 kilometres away. Rita is the pilot-in-command; it's her job to fly the plane, keep her eyes on the sky, and make the final decisions. Avani handles communications and navigation; her focus is inside the cockpit, on managing sensors, performing checks, and making radio calls. After taking off, they have an embarrassing discussion with Central Tower about the typos on their flight plan. Avani's stomach flips, but Rita laughs it off. They make a request to climb to their scheduled cruising altitude and, once there, wait to be cleared en route to their destination. Tower approves their flight path and wishes them well. Avani switches to the next radio frequency, and they're off.

The cloud ceiling is low, and they decide to climb higher for maximum visibility. As they level out, they begin normal in-flight checks. It's all routine until they're interrupted by an incoming call from another plane in the zone. That plane's pilot reports that they're in a small vessel, doing training circles for practice in the area, coming downwind on the west side at an altitude that matches Avani and Rita's. To avoid a collision, Rita does a quick check with Avani then drops their altitude.

The other pilot contacts them again. It sounds like this other plane has also descended, though the pilot sounds confused about its exact position. The two students laugh at this other pilot's confusion (must be a rookie), discuss the new intel, and then Rita takes them higher again. Avani radios over their new location and this time receives an apology from the muddled pilot. The pilot explains that he's actually to the east of the airport they're flying over, too far away to worry about. Avani confirms that they have no conflict and resumes flight check. That's when she realizes that she didn't radio the local tower as they passed into this new air space. This is a significant error because radioing in is required by air regulations. Hanging her head and lost in thought, Avani feels sick when she thinks about how many marks this will cost them. Feeling a little defeated, she returns to the flight guide, looks up their destination airport, and begins to calculate when they'll need to report their approach. She doesn't want to make the same mistake twice.

Meanwhile, Rita has noticed that a yellow light on the console has started to flash. She's doesn't know what this indicates for this plane and begins to troubleshoot it. It's not red, and no sirens are going, so she knows it's not critical, but still... She should know what it means. She cross-checks gauges and tries a few adjustments, but the light remains on. Rita's attention is on the light, not the skies, and Avani is lost in thought, stressed about missing their air-space report. Rita asks for her help, and they agree they need to regroup.

They call the tower as required when they enter into the new controlled zone but realize they've forgotten to call for NAV Canada weather information. They confess this error and receive a wind report from an irritated controller. Avani is calculating wind direction and speeds and runway positions when Rita notices her altimeter has inexplicably failed. She realizes this was what the flashing yellow light was indicating and sighs. She pulls out the safety manual to investigate the location of the altimeter and then finds it – smack it in the middle of the console.

Relieved, Rita navigates around to line up with the runway. She asks Avani to begin landing checks and the usual protocols. Landing gear down, flaps open, and wouldn't you know it, another yellow light flashes. But they're cleared to land...so Rita makes the decision to stick with the plan. She begins their descent as Avani scrambles to figure out what this new light means. Rita isn't registering the windsock warning, and Avani fails to explain that she hasn't calculated the strength of the crosswinds. She doesn't know if their plane can handle it.

It can't.

But, luckily for Rita and Avani, this particular flight was all part of a well-constructed practice exercise in a sophisticated flight simulator that I had the good fortune to help facilitate. If I had to name the highlight of my career so far, this would be it. Using a simulated exercise led by Deanna Wiebe (a wonderful teacher and now chair of our Aviation Department) and working alongside Sonya Flessati (a fellow psychologist and one of my favourite people), I help pilots keep their cool when things go wrong in the air.

Now, most of us won't have to deal with these kinds of high-risk complications, but we can relate to them. Small things go wrong, and it throws you off track. Then you miss something else, and you feel frustrated. Maybe you're feeling irritated about the muddled people around you and fail to notice that you've missed something else.

Communication goes downhill when we're worried. Our decision-making ability is impaired when we feel impatient or annoyed.

In this scenario, Rita and Avani were actually safe at all times. It was a simulator, so no crash was possible, but there was a solution to each of the issues they faced, and they had more time than they realized. They could have stayed in the circuit above the airport until their calculations were complete and the new yellow light was decoded. And once they realized the winds were too strong to land in, they could have overshot the runway and then discussed the pros and cons of requesting an alternative runway or returning home.

Invariably, students forget these options because they feel rushed. It becomes hectic in the cockpit: somebody doesn't consult; somebody doesn't share what they've seen; someone has a hunch but doesn't verbalize it; or someone talks too much. Assumptions are made. Details are missed. Frustration and confusion ensue.

What's particularly fun about this kind of training is that Deanna creates distractions until the team gets flustered, and then we pause the scenario and talk about what's going on. We reflect on how stress impacts performance. Most students don't see it at first – they don't know what they've missed, because stress causes a sort of tunnel vision (while from the outside, we can see more of the big picture). We then teach them some stress-management strategies to use when everything starts to go wrong and then let them finish the scenario with this new insight and wisdom.

The success that follows comes from them using resources more efficiently. We encourage them to slow down, return to their checklists, and go back to their strengths. We normalize the experience of being pulled out of yourself when you're worried. That's what stress does! It blinds us – and we flip to less effective ways of managing information. We maybe get stuck on a detail or worried about something far in the future. Quiet people start talking, extroverts go silent. Some of us tend to blame others for what's going wrong, or we get stuck on the mistake we made five minutes ago that is no longer relevant to what we're facing now.

When we slow things down, analyze the information we have, and consult with those around us, we make better choices. When we're calmer, we also feel safe. In these pilot-training sessions, they're always safe, and in school you'll (mostly) be safe too, even though you're feeling stressed. Each challenge will likely have a solution. The stress will bring out some of your worst personality traits (blaming others, acting in haste, being distracted), but as you learn about how you react to stress, you can adjust. In a counselling setting, we teach students how to assess for safety and then calm their systems down.

Step 1 = Safety
Step 2 = Soothing
Step 3 = Solution

Step 1: Are You Safe?

If you aren't safe, then you need to seek help immediately.

If it's a physical situation – call 911, get help, and move to a safe place as soon as you can.

If you're facing a crisis and suicide is on your mind, then please put down this book and call the suicide hotline for support (1-800-SUICIDE). If you can't keep yourself safe right now, please call 911 for help. It's important that you not be alone through this.

If you're feeling emotionally threatened by someone else, then you also need help. Talk with someone you trust who can connect you with practical resources and provide you with emotional support.

If your life is not in danger, but your grades are – then read on for tips about how to deal with classes.

URGENT TIP

If you're in distress and would like to talk with someone about mental health issues, you can always reach out to Canada's free Crisis Text Line (crisistextline.ca). Send a text to 686868 and connect with English- and French-speaking crisis responders, 24/7.

Step 2: If You're Safe but Stressed Out ... Soothe First

If you're safe (there are no threats around you, no hazards) but you're freaking out (you don't feel safe, you're in distress), then we need to soothe the body and bring it back to a calm state before we can figure out what's going on. Your system is currently overwhelmed, and we need to bring you back into balance to let the trigger subside.

PLEASE REMEMBER – if there's an ACTUAL DANGER, you need to deal with that first. If there's no immediate threat, then soothe yourself the best you can and get back into the business of solving the problem.

Recognize Your Stress Response

During times of high stress, we all tend to think in circles (sometimes we literally walk around in them). You know it's inefficient to panic, and yet that's what often happens.

What's your personality like when things go horribly wrong? Let's say you're facing a term-paper deadline that you're not prepared for.

- Do you say "screw it" and head to your mini-bar or an online essay farm? (I'm going to assume that you know these options are unwise: the first is ineffective, and the second will get you kicked out of school.)

- Or are you a stress extrovert who needs to talk it through with your closest friend until you can form a plan?

- Will you curl up in a corner and hope that tomorrow brings some new insight, that the cobbler elves will work on your paper overnight and you'll wake up in the morning and, Voilà!, you'll discover five pages of a well-referenced work waiting for you?

- Or will you pull a desperate all-nighter and try to pull your grade out of the fire?

There are good reasons to be stressed out (money issues, health problems, demanding schedules, or flashing yellow lights on your dashboard). Life is full of things we care about (or, at least, I hope it is), and it makes sense to feel stress when one of those things is threatened or damaged in some way.

It's almost guaranteed that something will go wrong for you while you're in university (life stuff), and at some point, you're going to hit the wall with essays, exams, and other deadlines (university stuff). When too many of these things happen at once, well, that's what we mean by #@%&! hitting the fan. It's a messy business.

Consider this scenario: It's 3:00 a.m., and you're feeling desperate. You've already sent an overshare email to your prof trying to explain why yesterday's term paper won't be in tomorrow. Your best friend is pissed at you because you cancelled a get-together at the last minute (having forgotten you said you'd be there), and you're wondering how you can give yourself the flu to get out of Wednesday's exam. Your place is a mess, but luckily your roommate hasn't noticed... they're caught up in their own chaos. This is crunch time, and you can feel the pressure weighing down on you.

What should you do first? Review for the quiz? Start the assignment? Do more research for the essay? Watch a cat video? Call your mom?

Given the hour, it's best not to call Mom right now – but you could absolutely reach out to her in the morning. For now, as insane as it seems, it makes sense to either get some sleep or make a plan to address the thing with the highest priority. Before you move into that step, you'll have to put a few things on hold and calm your system down so you can think clearly.

Bring on the Parasympathetic Response

Hysterical people have a hard time solving problems. You're likely not feeling hysterical, exactly, but if you're at your wit's end and you're upset, mad, or petrified – then we have to deal with that emotional response first and then move on to solving the issue. The one must come before the other. It's brain science.

You've probably heard of the fight-or-flight stress response? Well, the parasympathetic response is the opposite of that. It's sometimes called the relaxation response or the rest-and-refresh response. All of these responses are driven by our autonomic nervous system – they're hard-wired into each of us. We all have a sympathetic branch for the stress response and its opposite – the parasympathetic branch for the relaxation response.

Ideally, we spend most of our lives guided by parasympathetic functioning: we're breathing calmly, digesting our food well, and experiencing regular blood flow and circulation. When we're at ease, we learn better, laugh more, remember more, and relate better. It's the part of our system that aims for health and a long life.

But if you're walking through the woods and encounter a dangerous situation – a bear, let's say – you don't want to focus on rest and relaxation. You want to take swift action to save your life. This is where the sympathetic branch comes in.

The sympathetic branch fires up when you feel threatened. It gives you an immediate surge of energy to protect against the danger. It's called the "fight-flight-freeze response" because it drives us to one of those survival mechanisms. The sympathetic response floods our system with adrenalin and cortisol, giving us a bit more power to fight off the threat. Blood rushes to the largest muscles in our body to help us run away or, if the threat is intense and inescapable, we might shift into a last-ditch effort to save our lives by becoming so scared that we can't move.

This stress response is designed to save our lives when we're threatened. But we don't need it when we're freaking out about deadlines. We don't need to focus on saving our lives; we just need to bring the body back into a parasympathetic state.

How do you do that?

- If you're overactivated (fighting or fleeing) and/or in an overheated state (hyper-arousal): cool your system down by drinking some cold water and slowing your breathing.

- If you're so scared that you're freezing up (hypo-arousal): warm up your body by doing some cardio or drinking something warm.

The aim, in either case, is to bring your body back into the window of tolerance so you can work through the problem in front of you using a well-designed response rather than a quick fear-based reaction.[1]

If it's been a while, or if it was a crappy meal (and, no, Red Bull is not considered a food group), have a bite of something to settle your stomach. Eat something high in protein, and take a few more deep breaths. These actions will also help you re-engage your parasympathetic response, which will eventually help you to reduce your stress reaction.

Step 3: Seek a Solution

Once you're a bit calmer, assess how much time you have left to resolve the problem. If you have more than eight hours, then you might want to spend some of that time sleeping. Sleep is the number one thing you can do for your long-term health. Getting seven to nine hours of continuous sleep each night can even improve your lifespan, but in the short-term, sleep also improves your cognitive functioning. With a little sleep, you'll write clearer sentences, you'll remember what you studied with greater accuracy, and you'll be less prone to distraction and emotional reactivity. An hour of work done by a well-rested student will produce superior results compared to three hours of work from an exhausted student.

My best friend, research associate, and life partner is a professor of computing and, in that field, undergraduates routinely work through the night trying to solve a bug on an assignment. It's a bit of a rite of passage for students learning programming to fall asleep at their keyboards at 2:00 a.m., 3:30 a.m., or 5:00 a.m. – distraught at the "damn bug that just won't go away."

Hating their computers, these students nod off still being stuck on the problem. But then, upon waking, with almost no effort, they'll find themselves solving that bug in under five minutes. Programmers from San Francisco to Shanghai will tell you stories of this happening to them.

If your school tasks will benefit from clear thinking tomorrow –
then get some sleep now.

Sleeping on it won't make your deadlines go away, but it will make you more effective at meeting them. If you're thinking about pulling an all-nighter, or a late–late-nighter, the next chapter is especially for you.

Key Messages

☆ It's common in university to feel like you're going to crash and burn, but most of the time you're safer than you realize. Sometimes, when the stress of school is very high and our resources seem very low, thoughts of quitting school or quitting life may enter our minds. If you're feeling suicidal, then you must talk with someone about those feelings. University student services are remarkably supportive; please reach out and use them. If it's late at night, and you need to talk to someone, use this helpline: 1-833-456-4566. Or text 686868.

☆ Our communication and assessment skills go downhill when we're worried. If you're not currently in danger but you're feeling scared, soothe the body first – then tackle the problem.

☆ When you're feeling emotionally overwhelmed, focus on engaging the parasympathetic nervous system, or the relaxation response.

☆ Once you're feeling calm, assess the deadlines you're facing and, if possible, get some sleep.

11

ALL-NIGHTERS AND
LATE-LATE-NIGHTERS

I'm freaking out. Should I pull an all-nighter? Can I get an extension?
Does cramming for an exam pay off?
What happens if I hand something in late?

IF YOUR DEADLINE is less than eight hours away and you still have more than a few hours of work left, then you may feel pressured to burn the midnight oil, stay up until 4:00 a.m., or maybe even pull an all-nighter. How do you know when the loss of sleep is worth it?

Staying up through the night to get things done is never the preferred strategy. Your work will be subpar (not your best stuff), and the next day will be almost a total write-off (you're going to feel heavy and nauseous).

I pulled an all-nighter once or twice in my undergrad, and I've pulled dozens of late–late-nighters throughout my career – even during the process of writing this book. I'm the kind of person who gets a lot of energy as the end approaches, and sometimes my thoughts are more focused when I'm under the pressure of a deadline. I'm also always working on a variety of things, and sometimes deadlines sneak up on me (I've either procrastinated or just been so disorganized I forgot they were coming). In any case, I've spent many late nights working to get things in, mostly with successful outcomes. It's not the best way of working, but it's not the worst thing either – so long as it doesn't happen often and so long as you follow some simple rules.

The Rules
If you're going to pull a late-nighter (2:00 a.m.), a late–late-nighter (4:00 a.m.), or an all-nighter (self-evident), here are the rules you'll need to follow to make it successful:

QUICK FACT 📢
Just one all-nighter can decrease your reaction time by 300 percent, and staying up for twenty-two hours (pulling a late-nighter) is the equivalent of having four alcoholic drinks.[1]

1. *Never pull one to prepare for an exam.*
My performance on exams (and likely yours, too) is MUCH, MUCH better if I've had at least six hours of sleep. Research shows that I'm not alone. Moderate sleep deprivation produces impairments on par with alcohol intoxication. It's like being drunk, which is no way to approach an exam. Sleep deprivation will mess up your mind; you'll forget easy things and make stupid mistakes. Don't cram all night for a test! Sleep instead, and then get up early and study on a rested brain.

2. *No alcohol.*
Drinking alcohol will only slow you down, and if you can afford to slow down, then you might as well sleep.

3. *No heavy work the next day.*
That is, no road trips or long drives and no practicum shifts in hospital. The day after a late-nighter or all-nighter is going to be awful. Keep your expectations low on what you'll be able to do.

4. *Only stay up late if your deadline is before noon.*
If tomorrow's deadline is beyond noon – say 4:30 p.m.... or midnight the next night – then it's better to get some sleep and get up early to work through the day. Do a long all-dayer instead of a late–late-nighter.

5. *Only stay up late if the marks are worth it.*
This is a hard thing for undergrads to get their head around, and it takes a bit of calculating, but you need to know how valuable the deadline is and what the penalties are for being late or for missing the assignment altogether.

Do's and Don'ts for the Late-Late-Nighter		
Yes	**Limit**	**Avoid**
• Water and snacks	• Music	• Television
• Stretching often	• Cellphone use	• Working in bed
• Blankets and pillows	• Caffeine (weird but true)	• Texting or chats
		• Gaming
• Desk with good lighting	• Negative self-talk	• Alcohol
	• Background reading	• Multi-tasking
• Focus on the task		

To see how these rules work in practice, let's look at some examples.

Fatima's Dilemma

Fatima is facing a deadline for an assignment that's worth 25 percent of her final grade. She has finished an outline, but she still has about twelve hours of work left to get it ready to hand in. She had planned to work on it over the weekend, but her family requested her help at home, so she didn't get anything done. She's back in residence now, Sunday at 8:00 p.m., and the paper is due in class tomorrow at 9:00 a.m. She's been an A student up to this point, and she's never pulled an all-nighter. Should tonight be the night?

Here are her choices. What should she do?

A. Stay up until 4:00 a.m. then sleep until 7:00 a.m. Edit the assignment and hand it in at 9:00 a.m., even if it's not done.

B. Work until 11:00 p.m. then sleep until 5:00 a.m. Do as much as possible before 9:00 a.m. then hand it in.

C. Stay up until it's done then hand it in at 9:00 a.m. Sleep through the day.

D. Email the professor and explain that it's not done. Ask for an extension. Go to sleep and see what happens in the morning.

E. Go to bed now (it's 8:00 p.m.) and wake up at 4:00 a.m. Do as much as possible and hand it in at 9:00 a.m.

F. Check the course outline to see what the late penalty is. Consider the other deadlines coming up this week and then decide what to do next.

Did your opinion of what to do change as you read through those options? Most students don't think about checking the late penalties. They're so focused on needing to get things done that they forget to consider the facts of the situation when weighing the options.

Even a paper worth 25 percent is NOT worth a late–late-nighter if the late penalty is only 1 percent per day. The late factor becomes more important if the penalty is 10 percent. Do you see where we're going with this?

In Fatima's case, the course outline stated that late papers lose 2 points per day out of a possible 25. She estimated that if she had twelve good hours of focused time on that paper, she could keep her A average and land a mark of about 23/25. If she lost 2 points for one day late, then her mark would be 21/25.

Was twelve hours possible? Well, if she stayed up until 2:00 a.m., she could get four good hours in, maybe five, and she would have to work through most of the next day to finish it off. She thought it was doable.

The other option would be to stay up all night, knowing that her work wouldn't be as great as it would be on a good night's sleep. She figured she could push to get a grade of about 19/25 or 20/25.

In either case, she figured that she'd lose out on the next day. She'd either be working on the paper, or she'd be exhausted and feeling ill.

Fatima decided to launch into the assignment and reassess her progress later that night. She used the working-in-layers method (see Marcel's example beginning on page 143) and felt she'd completed an assignment worth about 15/25 by 1:00 a.m.

Feeling okay about that, she set her alarm for 7:00 a.m. and got about six hours of sleep. She reviewed her work in the morning and decided that it would be worth taking the late penalty and putting in the extra effort through the day to produce a better paper. As it turns out, in the 9:00 a.m. class, the prof said they could have an extension until 4:00 p.m. (Love it when that happens!) She was both annoyed and relieved by this news. She took the rest of the day to finish it and handed in a paper that earned a grade of 22/25.

> **QUICK TIP ϟ**
> If you stayed up later than usual, check your work for fatigue-related errors. Read your written stuff aloud and listen for mistakes or send it to a friend for early-morning proofing if you can.

Put the "Late Paper" in Perspective

As Fatima's example shows, sometimes handing in a decent paper a few days late is better than handing in a half-baked version on time.

If your paper is worth 20 percent and you hand in a crappy version where you're likely to get 40 percent – then you're walking away with 8/20 towards your final mark.

If you wait two days and complete a decent paper worth a grade of 70 percent – then you're earning 14/20.

The tipping point is the late penalty.

If you lose 10 percent a day (or in this case 2 points out of 20) and you're two days late – then you might end up with 10/20 on that same 70 percent paper…Is that worth two days of your time and stress? The answer might be no – it might be better to hand it in as a 40 percenter or to split the difference and take just one extra day with the hope of passing the assignment.

Let four key questions guide your decision:

1. How much is the assignment/paper worth? Not what it's graded out of but how much it's *worth* for the overall mark. CHECK THE COURSE OUTLINE. If in doubt, talk to your professor (or the teaching assistant).

2. Can you fail the paper and still pass the class? Do you need to pass every element in the class, or is it okay to fail or miss a piece of the course? How are your other grades right now? Could you afford to miss this assignment altogether? CHECK THE COURSE OUTLINE.

3. What is the late penalty on this assignment/paper? CHECK THE COURSE OUTLINE.

4. Is it possible to get an extension and avoid that late penalty? ASK THE PROFESSOR. If you are in over your head and unable to meet your deadlines, talk with your professor about your options. If your professor knows you (because you've been going to class and asking questions), then they may be more likely to give you some flexibility when things go wrong. Of course, they could say no, or they could ask you to seek support through counselling or your doctor's office. If they do, that's okay. Support from others might be good right now, and if the professor can't give you an extension, at least you know what you're facing.

Jake's Dilemma

If your assignment is worth a small amount of the total, if you don't have to pass all things in the course to pass the entire class, and if you've had good marks to this point, then maybe it makes strategic sense to not do that paper.

This is what Jake is wondering, but he's going to have to do the math to make the decision. If Jake doesn't hand in this assignment, what kind of grade would he need on the final to pass the course?

Let's walk through it.

According to the course syllabus, Jake's class has six elements that make up the final grade: three assignments, a group project, and two exams. The course syllabus includes a note: "An overall passing grade of 60 percent is required for second-level courses. There's no requirement here to pass each element of this course."

The breakdown looks like this:

Assignment 1	10
Assignment 2	10
Midterm exam	20
Group project	20
Assignment 3	10
Final exam	30
Total (%)	100

Jake's been doing well in the course so far. He draws a table to assess his standing in the class.

Course element	Weight	Jake's grade
Assignment 1	10	70% = 7/10
Assignment 2	10	80% = 8/10
Midterm exam	20	85% = 17/20
Group project	20	80% = 16/20
Assignment 3	10	?
Final exam	30	?
Total (%)	100	48/100

Based on what he's done so far, he's running an 80 percent average, but if he were to stop now and NOT do Assignment 3 or the final exam his final mark would only be 48 percent. That's a fail.

Scenario A: Bare Pass

Jake could skip the assignment and aim for a bare pass. What would he need to get on the final exam to pass the course with a final grade of 60 percent?

To pass the course (with a grade of 60 percent), he needs 12 more points – either from Assignment 3 or the final exam. If he doesn't get any of those points from the assignment, then he'll need to get them on the final exam. That exam is worth 30 percent – so he needs 12/30, or 40 percent.

Course element	Weight	Jake's grade
Assignment 1	10	7/10
Assignment 2	10	8/10
Midterm exam	20	17/20
Group project	20	16/20
Assignment 3	10	0/10
Final exam	30	12/30 = (40%)
Total (%)	100	60/100

Jake has done so well on the other elements of the course that he's set himself up with a nice buffer. In his case, he could miss the 10 percent assignment completely and even fail the final exam with a grade of 40 percent, and STILL PASS THE COURSE.

Now, is this the most desirable outcome? No, of course not, but it reduces his stress to see this chart. He feels confident now because no matter what happens on his assignment, he's unlikely to fail the class.

Scenario B: A Clear Pass
Jake could skip the assignment and aim for a decent final exam grade.

Course element	Weight	Jake's grade
Assignment 1	10	7/10
Assignment 2	10	8/10
Midterm exam	20	17/20
Group project	20	16/20
Assignment 3	10	0/10
Final exam	30	21/30 = (70%)
Total (%)	100	69/100

This is a realistic estimate: a final exam grade that isn't as strong as his midterm but is still in line with his overall performance. A 70 percent grade on the final exam would give him 21 points out of the 30 possible. When added to his existing 48 points – that brings him to 69 percent.

This is a clear pass, even with a 0 on Assignment 3.

Scenario C: A Decent Final Grade
Jake sees that if he gets just one more percentage point in the course, he could push into the next letter grade. Instead of a C+, he would have a B- in the course. One percentage point is only 1 out of 10 on his assignment. Could he get a 10 percent on Assignment 3?

Let's say he decides to hand in a sloppy, half-finished assignment: he does a few questions and skips others. He estimates that he could get a 30 percent on Assignment 3 without much stress. He leaves a note for his professor admitting he didn't put too much effort into the project but wanted to hand in what he could under the circumstances.

Let's see how this might play out.

Course element	Weight	Jake's grade
Assignment 1	10	70% = 7/10
Assignment 2	10	80% = 8/10
Midterm exam	20	85% = 17/20
Group project	20	80% = 16/20
Assignment 3	10	3/10 = (30%)
Final exam	30	21/30 = (70%)
Total (%)	100	72

Jake feels more confident after running these numbers because he's pretty sure he can pull off a final exam mark that's better than 70 percent. He also sees that handing in a half-assignment is better than skipping it altogether. A few percentage points can swing his final grade from a C+ to a B- or from a B- to a B+.

The Strategic Decision

Jake decides to submit the assignment half-done, and he is now motivated to keep focused on the final push through exams.

If you're facing a similar situation, I encourage you to take out your course syllabus and run the numbers before you pull an all-nighter or a late–late-nighter. If running the numbers seems complicated, then trust that you'll be able to think clearly through the details and form an effective strategic plan with a little bit of sleep.

I bet a counsellor or an academic advisor could also help you with these calculations. This is the kind of math I do in counselling sessions with students all the time.

Key Messages

☆ Staying up all night to get things done is never the "preferred" strategy.

☆ Never pull a late–late-nighter if you're studying for an exam. Your mind will be mushy, your performance subpar.

☆ Performance on exams is significantly improved by six hours of sleep.

☆ The Late–Late-Nighter Rule Recap:

> Never pull one to prepare for an exam.

> No alcohol.

> No heavy work the next day.

> Only stay up late if your deadline is before noon.

> Only stay up late-late if the marks are worth it.

☆ Late–late-nighters might make sense if your deadline is before noon. If your deadline is later in the day, then get some sleep and do a long all-dayer instead of a late–late-nighter.

☆ When making decisions about burning the midnight oil, ask yourself these four questions:

> How much is the thing worth?

> Can I fail this thing and still pass the class?

> What is the late penalty?

> Is it possible to get an extension to avoid the late penalty?

☆ Sometimes it makes sense (and it's okay) to hand in a half-done assignment.

☆ If the late penalty is small, then a late–late-nighter likely isn't worth it. Finishing the project on a good night's sleep will likely give you a better outcome.

MANAGING THE STRESS
AND COPING WITH
OUTSIDE DISTRACTIONS

I'm constantly exhausted, what can you suggest to help?
I'm bogged down by stress, how can I bolster my mental health?
How do I manage unexpected life crises, and still get my shit done for school?

I'M GETTING a grip on school, but I'm distracted by other problems. I'm worried about my family, money, relationships, adulting. How do I fit the rest of my life in around school work? These concerns are the kinds of things that bring students into my counselling office.

I'm confident that at some point during your first year of university, you'll get a handle on the school stuff. You'll become more syllabus-savvy – able to keep track of deadlines and make sense of what each professor wants. The thought of an assignment or midterm won't be as intimidating. You'll be able to bang out a journal entry when you need to, and you'll know that there are resources out there to help you with a research paper if you need them. You'll know where the library is, what your student ID card is good for, and where to go when you need to eat, find a friend, or grab a moment to yourself.

But that doesn't mean that student life is easy.

I know it's not.

Just because school feels more doable doesn't mean that you'll have an easy ride through the rest of the term. Life happens along-side school, and with life come successes and setbacks, love and loss, worries and strains. Once you realize that you *can* do the work, when to do it becomes the challenge. How will you fit it all in around all the other stuff you have going on in your life? There's a sea of details that are easy to drown in…Who needs what? When is that due? What time was I supposed to be there? Where are we meeting? What time is my shift?

To manage financial stress, most students are employed while they go to school. Working as baristas, bartenders, or servers or in security, coaching, child care, retail sales, or recreation is common. Later, you might find career-related jobs are easier to find – for instance, research assistantships, lab positions, residence advising, peer support, professional aid (e.g., teaching, nursing, athletic therapy), or departmental positions doing marketing, outreach, social networking, or community work.

The ugly parts of university life will also be draining. You may encounter racism, misogyny, bigotry, homophobia, or other forms of injustice. You may be tired of being called upon to represent "your people," and you may be angry about "having to educate" professors and classmates about the impacts of systemic racism. Having to step up or step in to these spaces can take a toll on our energy and our mental health.

Other parts of life can be draining too. Family responsibilities don't end just because we're in university. You might have parents, or even children, counting on you for support. If you attend university in your home town, you might find yourself driving siblings to sports or music lessons, or you might be expected to "leave school behind" when you walk through the front door – expected to cook, clean, organize, and converse like you did before university took over. You might have athletic interests that require your time: a team may be counting on you, a trainer may have expectations of you, or you may have your own desire to keep yourself moving and in shape.

Volunteering is another thing students often try to fit in. Increasingly, we're seeing programs (such as psychology, social work, business, public relations, early childhood development, and nonprofit studies) that require students to have experience in their field of interest. Many graduate school applications ask for evidence of community involvement and volunteerism.

Finally, relationships, friendships, and family time are likely very important to you. You'll want to spend time with your best friends, but you'll find social time is sometimes hard to fit in. Whether it's Marvel movies, a D&D campaign, bar hopping, hiking, or a trampoline park…you'll likely want more time for it. How do successful students manage these multiple demands? Here are some proven strategies I've seen that withstand the test of time.

Take Intentional Breaks to Sharpen Your Saw

Let's start at the source – that's you – and what you bring to the table. This will make a huge difference in how well you feel and how efficiently you operate.

The writer Stephen Covey, in his *7 Habits of Highly Effective People,* tells the story of a lumberjack, and I'm going to modify it to make a point.[1] Let me also add a disclaimer: I'm not advocating for the clear-cutting of forests, and I recognize that this story has roots in the colonial tradition. Still, I love this story and draw from it often. Here it goes:

Once upon a time, a lumberjack worked hard in the forest to cut down a tree. He used one of those three-foot crosscut saws that required full-body engagement. He threw himself back and forth, determined to get the job done, to cut through that tree for firewood. Along came another lumberjack, who paused to watch him at work.

After observing for a minute or so, she said, "Hey, looks like you're not getting too far on that trunk."

"Yeah, this blade is really dull."

"Why don't you stop and sharpen it then?" she said.

"Can't," he said. "No time. Got to get this done." He continued to work, harder and harder, and he got nowhere but tired.

Of course, if he had paused, sharpened his saw, and then went back to work with a renewed tool, he'd have progressed with more ease and less stress. But this isn't the way we're wired. When we're working towards deadlines, we're often blind to logic. Take a break and go back when you're sharp. You'll save yourself a lot of stress, and the task will take a fraction of the time.

I'm assuming that as a student you're not cutting down trees (though you might consume a lot of paper), so when I say sharpen your saw, I mean take a break to sharpen your mind.

Consider Ewan. He says he takes breaks all the time. He stops to check his phone, goes to the bathroom, checks his phone again, uploads a baby squirrel photo. None of that sharpens his saw. Most micro-breaks are actually energy-wasters. They distract us but don't sharpen us. To sharpen your saw, take intentional breaks to re-energize your mind. Take a break and get some sleep. Go out with your friends. Go for a run, or lose yourself in a movie. Take a break and let your mind rest. When you return to your task, you'll feel sharper. You'll get it done faster, and likely better – and you'll enjoy the work more.

But as a student we often say, "Can't, no time," "Got to get this done," and we keep slogging away at reduced capacity, taking distracting micro-breaks that get us nowhere. We think we're working efficiently, but we're not.

Work in Layers, Not Columns

Working in layers rather than columns will help you build a safety net to protect yourself against the unexpected. If something gets in the way of your school work, you'll still have something to hand in. I'm including this strategy of working in layers because it will help you build resilience. It's one that Marcel, a first-year English student, came to appreciate the hard way.

Marcel is the kind of guy who takes things in stride. He's laid-back but also feels motivated to get things done. He likes to be methodical with course work, moving one step at a time through each week. His approach to deadlines was linear. Whatever was due next was the thing he was working on. Finish that up and then move on to the next thing. Many students take this approach. They look at their deadlines – hopefully all spelled out on a calendar that they can see easily – and they work on what's next on the list. When Marcel had five deadlines in two weeks, he focused on the first assignment first – and when it was done, he moved on to the next thing.

I call this the *column approach*. If you're working on an essay, then you start from scratch and build it up into a written masterpiece. The column gets higher as the essay gets better and better. You work on the first task until it's in great shape, and then you work on the next thing until it reaches that level too. When it's done, you move on to the third task, and so on. If you're a sophisticated academic, then this column process is excellent. It allows for focused productivity and promotes closure on projects. However, for newer learners (like most first-year students) and those working with multiple, competing deadlines (like most first-year students)...the column strategy leaves you vulnerable to the unexpected. Further, if you're prone to perfectionism, the column strategy might trap you into working on one paper that never seems to get done. You want that column to be built up as high as it can go, so you fail to move on to the other things on your list.

Perfectionism was not a barrier for Marcel, though. He aimed for solid work, and he was feeling good about his pacing and his progress. Until his girlfriend broke her leg. As her driver, Marcel's time was taken up getting her to and from appointments and waiting for her classes to end so they could head home together. He finished his first two assignments and got started on his first big paper, but then he ran out of time. The second paper wasn't even started, and the report was not even on his radar.

Marcel was granted an extension for one paper and took late penalties on the others, but these extensions had a cascading effect. His next set of deadlines was affected, and he felt rushed on everything. If he maintained his column approach, more work would be left undone.

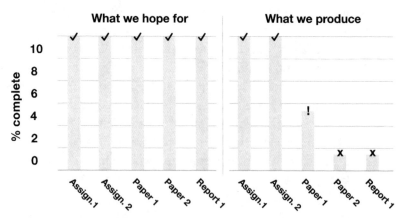

After some consultation and soul searching, Marcel decided to take a different approach. He switched strategies and began *working in layers*. He still had five deadlines to meet, but he looked at them as a whole package rather than as individual events. In the layer method, you work across tasks, not one at a time. You're trying to create balance and stability in a system resilient to threats.

This is Marcel's advice for approaching these deadlines:

- Create an outline for each assignment, paper, or report.

- Sketch out a crappy first draft for each one, using point-form lists for the assignments and mind maps for the papers.

- Revise and refine the drafts. Transform those point-form lists into decent paragraphs. Expand on the mind maps, add details and provide evidence by doing library research, and draft a thesis statement. Put in just enough work for a passing grade.

- Go back and work a bit more on each thing, bringing everything up to a solid B level, starting with the thing that is worth the most.

- Time permitting, go back again and bring everything up to an A level, starting with the thing that's worth the most.

Marcel brought the two papers up to a B level, but then he began to run out of time. He decided the reports weren't worth as much, so he put less effort into them and switched his focus back to the papers. He figured he got one of them up to an A level … maybe both.

The good thing about layers is that it gives you a strategy for managing the unexpected. Even if Marcel had run out of time before he could polish his papers, he felt confident about them – they were ready. At the "good" level, they weren't his best work, but they were in solid shape nonetheless. Marcel felt safe using this approach because if (or when) things fell apart, he had progress to share. He had set himself up to pass no matter what life threw his way.

He also found he could build in time to review his papers. He got some feedback from his partner about one of them and another

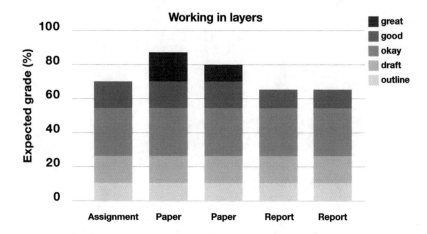

was reviewed by a classmate. He incorporated their suggestions on the next pass. Marcel says he recommends this strategy because it's crisis-resistant, and he felt the last-minute rush should be about achieving excellence, not preventing failure.

As you go on, you'll find that the drawback of the layers approach is that it requires you to switch between tasks and divides your attention. You never fully reach your potential on any one thing because you stretch yourself too thin. To mitigate these risks, be careful about how many things you take on at one time – three might be easier to handle than five, and seven is likely too many.

The Way of the Buffalo

Working in layers builds resilience, but you'll also need grit to get through some of the personal challenges that will come your way this year. In my experience, the majority of first-year students experience significant changes in their circle of friends and their love lives. Other strains can come from family situations and work stress. Under these kinds of strains, we can sometimes find strength outside ourselves. For me, it's been the buffalo.

Many years ago, when I was facing a personal crisis and was feeling afraid, I was told to think about the buffalo as a reminder of the need for strength and perseverance. Tasha Hubbard, an Indigenous scholar, said that Mandan-Hidatsa Elder Gerard Baker told her that the buffalo "represented strength, wisdom, fierceness and bravery, and the people believed that the buffalo taught them a lot."[2] Elder Roy Bear Chief told me the same thing. When a bad storm approaches, birds fly away and most animals run for cover, moving away from the thunder, sleet, snow, wind, or rain. Elder Bear Chief told me that cows try to outrun the storm, but they're too slow and often get caught up in it. People can sometimes be this way, too – getting caught up in a situation that they wish to avoid, hiding from conflict or pretending things are okay when they're actually not.

Every creature does what it can to avoid the storm…except the buffalo. When they sense a storm approaching, buffalos move towards it, knowing that the best way to cope with a crisis is to face it head-on. Picture the buffalo summoning its courage, lowering its head, and facing the threat directly. The Blackfoot word for "lowers its head" is Ayiiskoh kya kiya. Buffalo trust that they have the internal resources needed to endure the journey through the storm; they know they'll have an opportunity to recoup on the other side, under the clear skies that await them there.

We all face times of upheaval, disturbances of one kind or another. Some are brief, others long-lasting; some are tame, others wicked. As a psychologist, I've supported students as they've faced all kinds of storms, including school-related situations like exams, classroom presentations, competing deadlines, and high-conflict situations, but also personal storms related to grief, anxiety, depression, oppression, dilemmas, and pain. Many try to wait out these storms by delaying decisions or hoping circumstances will change; others try to avoid them or deny they're there. But the buffalo show another way – a way through. And most often, they walk through the storm together.

In the words of Elder Bear Chief, "the buffalo story is a good analogy for facing issues rather than running away from them. Some students do avoid or procrastinate." Whenever you can, gather your resources, stay close to your people, turn to face the storm, lower your head, and walk towards it. Walk through the storm to get to the other side. It's the fastest way to reach those sunny skies.

Don't Fence Yourself In

Since hearing about the way of the buffalo, I've been sensitive to other buffalo stories. One of my advisors, Elizabeth Lourens, described the buffalo as gentle herd animals who like to roam free. Gentle, that is, until they're fenced in. She told me that when a buffalo feels restricted, it will fight against the limits until it's free. She encouraged me to think about my inner buffalo, that part of myself that wants to roam in the open, free of restrictions. Our inner buffalo fights back when we're told we "can't do that" or we "shouldn't be that way." Sometimes, these messages come from the outside – from those around us; at other times, they are internal messages we send to ourselves.

Choosing to be free might mean liberating yourself from some of your expectations – the ways you fence yourself in or keep yourself locked up. You may also need to escape the hold of unhealthy situations – a bad job environment or an unhealthy relationship.

... But Have Some Boundaries

Allow yourself to roam free but have some boundaries. Spend time with people who help you feel amazing and limit the time you spend with people who make you feel like crap. Setting limits on your time and energy is important when you're feeling mentally exhausted, especially when your relationships are interfering with your ability to succeed in school.

Consider what happened to Betty. She entered the first year of her cultural studies program excited about what was ahead. It didn't take long for her to get bogged down in labs and assignments, tests and group projects. As she began to get a grip on managing what amounted to a sixty-hour work week, things at home blew up. She described the situation as a mega-fight that erupted after her eighteen-year-old sister, Faye, came home at 4:00 a.m. When her traditionally-minded parents threatened to disown Faye for her disobedience, Fay took her things and moved out. Betty's parents forbade her from contacting Faye, but she loved her and felt worried about her. She was also the only one who knew where Faye was staying (at her girlfriend's house), and she brought her personal items, clothing, and cash. She had been putting more hours in as a lifeguard at the pool, and between that and visiting Faye her studies began to suffer.

Is this a story about poor boundaries? Should Betty have said no to helping Faye so that she could put in the time to pass her biology course?

As you can imagine, there are no easier answers. Betty and Faye share a healthy attachment – they love one another – and with that connection comes responsibility. Although Betty was not responsible for Faye, she was committed to supporting her well-being. Though Faye may not have been thinking about it, I'm sure she was also committed to Betty's well-being. Building healthy boundaries sometimes means choosing between what's right for you and what's right for the person you love. If the relationship is toxic, then that sense of responsibility might not be shared or reciprocated, and your boundaries are going to be impacted by those circumstances.

In this case, Betty felt good about doing what she could to support Faye, but she also realized that taking care of Faye financially was going to be detrimental to her academic success. She wanted to encourage Faye to either work towards her own independence or make peace with their parents and come home. Betty's boundaries guided her to negotiate a plan that worked for both of them.

Now let's look at Frank. His situation was work-related and very different from Betty's. He took on a job as a bartender – not because he loved serving drinks but because he could make more each shift than anywhere else. The problem was – he hated it. He didn't like the music or the crowds it drew in. There were two staff members who got on his nerves constantly, and he found that he dreaded going in. He felt compelled to keep the job because the cash was undeniably good, and despite his efforts, he hadn't been able to land an alternative position.

Is this a case of having poor boundaries or just life?

Frank would say it was a bit of both. Feeling forced to maintain his position but also hoping to avoid conflict, he worked on what was in his power to change. Frank exercised his agency by asking for a different time slot, which meant he didn't have to work with the two people he found irritating. He learned more about the music he was listening to (which gave him more respect for it), and he started using earplugs to reduce the volume. He took an online mixology course that upped his skill level, and he encouraged a friend to apply for an associate position in the bar.

Even with positive companionship, more skills, ear plugs, and limited staff drama, Frank still didn't like the job. He stayed only for the money. It's the classic case of golden handcuffs ... he felt locked in because of the cash.

To escape, Frank set a savings goal – the amount of money he would need to carry him through to the end of term. When he reached it, he quit. The relief was immediate, and his enthusiasm for life tripled overnight. Frank's savings weren't quite enough to get through to May, but he did access the Emergency Loan program through his student union office, and then doors opened for him once he was available for full-time work in May. If you need financial resources, I'm sure your school has an emergency loan program, student bursaries, job boards, and employment supports.

Whatever you're facing, I encourage you to access the resources you need and work towards building boundaries that are right for you. Remember that there are counsellors on your campus who can help you untangle the issues and set your priorities – nice people like me available to help nice people like you.

Key Messages

☆ Just when you feel like you've got a grip on school stress, something else in your life will go sideways. The ugly parts of university can be draining too.

☆ Burnout takes many forms, but it's often associated with putting in great effort but not producing great results. If you're feeling this strain, it may be time to pause and refuel.

☆ Take a break to sharpen your mind – actual intentional breaks – no multi-tasking, no guilt.

☆ Learn to work in layers across projects rather than in columns. This strategy will help you manage the unexpected.

☆ If you want to change your state of distress, then you need to change your approach. Consider the buffalo as a metaphor for heading into, and through, the storm.

☆ Whatever you're facing, access resources on campus (and off) and work towards building boundaries that will preserve your mental health and well-being.

END IN SIGHT
BUT LOSING STEAM

I've lost my rhythm – how can I get back on track and finish off strong?
What happens if I can't finish the semester?
How do I withdraw from a class? And what does that do to my GPA?

YOU PROBABLY WON'T be surprised to hear that the demand for counselling appointments swells just as the end of the term comes into sight. At this point in the semester, students often feel that they can't focus any longer. They describe the feeling as being burned out, going in circles, mushy brain, or boredom. I often call it "hitting the wall," and I know it feels brutal.

FUN FACT
About 43 percent of marathon runners will hit the wall during a race.[1] Nearly every first-year student will hit the wall in November (and again in early March).

I use this phrase because students lose steam just like long-distance runners do. The road through the term is long, and keeping pace is challenging. Marathon runners talk about hitting the wall a few kilometres from the finish line, and they describe it as a gruelling mental (not physical) battle to get through to the finish line, especially if they're running that distance for the first time. In his book on running to win, George Sheehan states: "Eventually you learn that the competition is against the little voice inside you that wants you to quit."[2]

Somewhere around the thirty-second kilometre (that's about 75 percent of the way there, around the twenty-mile mark), you're going to want to give up. You're going to feel like stopping, and you'll be more tired than you ever imagined. In response to the question "What goes through your mind during the last mile of a marathon?," posted on Quora, runners responded:

> Any recreational runner that I know would say that the most challenging part of a marathon, mentally and physically, is in the 18–23-mile range, give or take. In that stage, you're getting exhausted, but you realize you still have around an hour left to go.
>
> The last few kilometres are like out-of-body experiences for many runners.
>
> Although you have not quite finished the race yet, you're coming to terms with what you have achieved and something that you have dedicated so much time and energy towards.[3]

Near the end of every term, students also tell me about feeling exhausted and wishing the semester were over, even though there are still several weeks and many exams to go. Jenny was no marathon runner, but when she was approaching the last hill of her semester, she felt like she was pushing through mud, managing cramps, self-doubt, exhaustion, and the desire to just give up. She wasn't alone (though she sure felt that way).

The biggest obstacle at this time of year is exhaustion. There have been so many deadlines and pressures related to school and life in general that there's a desire to just get it over with.

But in reality, Jenny didn't have that much left. She was more than three-quarters of the way through, and she'd come too far to give up. She'd be finished classes in about two weeks, and the heavy-lifting was mostly behind her. But she did have five final exams to get through and at least two assignments that needed to be handed in before the end of term. She was struggling with feeling overwhelmed and bored at the same time. She was losing energy as she pushed towards the finish line. She wanted to be done. She was so very over this.

Luckily for Jenny, you don't need to be a marathoner to get through the term. In addition to the runners' advice, there are things you can do to change up the path ahead without getting disqualified from the race. When university students hit the wall, in addition to working on their mindset, fuel, and training (as we'd do with runners), I counsel them to consider what can be changed in their situation to help them succeed. What kinds of things can we add or remove that would help, and is there value in altering the race-course itself?

To do this, let's look at the volume and intensity of what's left in the term, and then make a plan to work through (or around) those things. Addressing burnout is easier to fix than Jenny might realize. As one runner remarked: "As the finish loomed into view I knew how long that stretch was, so I concentrated on getting to the next tree, or the next lamppost, or the next set of traffic lights. And that way, I got to finish in my goal time and without walking a step."[4]

Taking Stock

For a runner, those last kilometres loom long, but it's all a trick of the mind. They're no longer (or shorter) than the ones already conquered. Feelings change the way we perceive the world, and being exhausted makes everything seem worse. The secret to soaring over the end-of-semester wall is to gain an accurate picture of the obstacles. I work with my clients to write out and make clear the volume, weight, and intensity of each obstacle (that is, assignment or exam) ahead, and then we make a resource plan to address those challenges. Here's an example of how it's done.

Volume (What's Left to Do This Term?)

Use your calendar and plot out your remaining deadlines for the next few weeks (many free printable calendars are available online). Jenny had two assignments and five finals left. To get full participation marks in her English class, she needed to do two class readings and prepare discussion questions for class.

In addition to her course work, Jenny had a job interview and three appointments in her schedule, and she planned to work two shifts a week until the break. She had friend commitments and household chores, her mom's birthday was the following weekend, and before the end of term she wanted to go shopping, see a movie, and clean out her car. We wrote all of those commitments onto her calendar.

Weight (What Are Your Priorities?)

Next, look at your course outlines and confirm how much each task is worth.

Jenny's exams were worth 20 percent, 30 percent, 40 percent, 40 percent, and 45 percent. The assignments were worth 15 percent and 25 percent. If she participated in the remaining English classes, she'd earn an additional 2 percent.

Going to the final lectures in each of her classes was a priority.

Measuring the worth of things goes beyond grade impact to include other commitments, priorities, and pleasures. On the commitments side, Jenny had made plans to work through the next few weeks on a regular schedule. She didn't need the money for anything specific right away, but she felt obliged to help her boss and to show up for the team. She gave that a moderate weighting in terms of her priorities. The interview fell into the high-priority category because it might land her a practicum placement next semester. The appointments were less important, and she thought she could reschedule them if necessary.

Family was very important to Jenny. The birthday celebration for her mom was a surprise event, and many family members were going to it. She'd done a lot of the planning, and she was looking forward to it.

Although it sounds irrational, she also decided that going to that movie was a high priority. It was part of a series that was coming to a close, and she'd been looking forward to it for over a year. Cleaning out her car was important, but not necessary. After considering her priorities, she decided to postpone shopping and detailing her car until exams were over. We updated the calendar to reflect these decisions.

Next, we looked at blocks of time across each week when she could study, and we added those numbers into the calendar. On Mondays she had four solid hours available. On Saturdays she was free, but we didn't want to write that down as a twelve-hour study day. Instead we underestimated those blocks of time (e.g., we put down a full Saturday as only six hours of available study time, knowing that she could do more if she needed). I wanted to set Jenny up to succeed.

As we plotted, Jenny noticed that it would be ridiculous to spend time at work on the last weekend before the start of the exam period. With three finals the following week, work just couldn't be her priority. She'd have to move her two appointments too. She decided to cancel those two shifts and an earlier one as well, and so we crossed them off her calendar.

She thought the other two weekends would be fine and that her boss would be agreeable to the plan. She said she would use the movie as a reward for finishing classes, and she could see that she'd already have several study periods in before she went to the movie. She was also pleased to keep her hair appointment, and the party day was wide open. We talked about what she could delegate in terms of party prep and cleanup, and she felt it was manageable.

Intensity (What Does Each Thing Require?)

This is the last part, and I warned Jenny it could get messy. On a fresh sheet of paper, and starting with course requirements, Jenny walked through each thing she had coming due, and estimated how many hours she thought she would need to complete each task. We talked about it as if she were aiming to keep her marks steady (or slightly above) where they were. I encouraged her to pad her estimates to account for wasted time and the unexpected and so she'd have more time to increase her grades. A paper might need twelve hours of her time, while an assignment might only need two. Once we had a list of what was required, we plotted these tasks into her calendar in blocks of time, giving her a visual representation of what to focus on and when. A clear picture of her workload began to emerge.

Okay, it was actually an incredibly messy picture, but it was functional, and Jenny saw it as doable – that's the best part.

What's great here is that Jenny could see that she had adequate time in her schedule to study for exams. Her "full days" were penned in as only six hours, and she was optimistic that she could get in ten if she focused. She felt good about the assignment time and realized that cancelling her work shifts would be wise. Her stress about her psychology exam dissipated as she saw that she could spend a solid nineteen hours reviewing her materials.

The biggest takeaway for Jenny was that her stress levels would drop when her third exam was over – only sixteen days away. In that period, she'd have two major good things (the birthday party and the movie night), and she estimated having adequate hours for each of her exam preps. She'd left herself some wiggle room on those longer study days, and she saw that she could schedule a date night once her first three exams were out of the way. It all looked possible now.

Why It Works

Accurate assessment is an antidote to anxiety. As we've said before, be like the buffalo – face the storm and walk towards it. Look it in the eye, and you'll notice that what you're facing isn't insurmountable after all. Yes, you're exhausted, but this kilometre is no longer than the last, and you're almost at the end. It's a matter now of plotting out your path and taking it one day at a time to the end.

The other reason why this technique works is that it takes the "rush" out of the equation. When you can take the time crunch out of the situation, it won't feel like a crisis anymore. Slow down your thinking to allow your brain to function as the problem-solving machine it is, and then look at the facts of the situation. As you plot out the end of your term, you're going to see what you need to let go of and what you want to keep.

Slowing things down also helps to re-engage the parasympathetic nervous system – it turns off the stress response and puts us back into a state of rational thinking, allowing us to make better use of our frontal lobe, neocortex, and the higher-ordered thinking abilities of our species. Once you have plotted out the details of your last few weeks, you're going to feel more in control. The picture of what you have left will become clear as you focus on it.

Withdrawals and Deferrals

Sometimes when we're losing steam at end of term we just can't get back on track. Your university has several systems in place to support students in this kind of need. I'm going to review a few policies available at my university, but I don't know if all of them are universal across Canada. Your academic advisor will have all of these answers, or you can consult your university's calendar.

Exam Deferrals (Do You Have Several Finals on One Day?)
If you have three exams scheduled close to one another (e.g., back-to-back or three within twenty-four hours), you might be able to request an exam deferral. It's up to you to check your schedule for these kinds of conflicts. If you see a pinch point, check the university calendar to see if moving an exam is possible, or talk with your professor about writing the exam early.

You can also ask for a deferral or course extension for other reasons (e.g., illness, loss, or a significant mental health event). Again, check with your professor, the university calendar, a counsellor, or an academic advisor for details.

Withdrawals (Are You Failing a Course?)
Some universities allow you to withdraw from a course – up until a certain date. At my university, it's around the eleventh week of classes, but at other schools, it's the last day of class. Know your deadlines and do a realistic check on your progress before that deadline passes. If you're failing a course and can't realistically pull it out of the fire, then it's better to take a W in the course instead of an F. You don't get your tuition fees back, but you can save your GPA.

Some universities include midterm grades on your transcripts, but every university records your final grade. You might think that all universities calculate and show grades in the same way, but there's actually a lot of variation from coast to coast. Some schools record final grades as a percentage (say, 85 percent or 63 percent); others convert percentages into letter grades (say, A- or a C+). Most translate letter and percentage grades into a grade point average, or GPA. Knowing how to do these calculations is important, as Zayden's situation demonstrates.

Zayden's school uses a four-point grading system. In class, each assignment Zayden did was marked with a percentage grade (e.g., 55 percent), and those percentages were converted to letter grades.

Letter grade	Point value for grade
A	4.00
B	3.00
C	2.00
D	1.00
F	0.00

Each university has a policy that shows how percentages are converted into letters. Zayden's transcript lists a letter grade for each course, but there's also an overall GPA. Your transcript may look similar to Zayden's, and to understand it, you'll need to look for your university's grade table (like the one above), and you'll need your transcript (like the one below).

Zayden's transcript			
Course	Credit hours	Grade	Grade points
Biology	5	A	20
Biology lab	1	B	3
English	5	C	10
Mathematics	5	F	0
	16 (attempted)		33 total

Zayden took three courses this semester, Biology (lecture and lab), English, and Math. All of his lectures counted as 5 credit hours, and the lab counted as 1 credit hour, for a total of 16 attempted credit hours. To get his "grade points," he needed to change each letter grade into a numerical grade using his university's standard (e.g., A=4). To get the grade points for each class, he then multiplied that grade by the number of credit hours.

Calculating your GPA looks like this:

$$\frac{\text{Total points earned}}{\text{Total credits attempted}} = \text{Grade point average}$$

With an F on his transcript, Zayden earned only 33 total points, and he had finished all his classes, so the total credits attempted was 33. This left him with a GPA for that semester of 2.06. At my university, this would mean that Zayden was still in good academic standing, but just. He'd need to keep his GPA above 2.0.

$$\frac{\text{33 points earned}}{\text{16 credits attempted}} = 2.06 \text{ GPA}$$

But what if Zayden had withdrawn from his math course instead of failing it? His points earned would have been the same, but the denominator of the formula would be lowered. The math course would NOT be included as a "credit attempted." In this scenario, he has five fewer credits in the denominator, which boosts his GPA. Sometimes withdrawing is a solid academic choice to make.

$$\frac{\text{33 points earned}}{\text{11 credits attempted}} = 3.0 \text{ GPA}$$

Most universities will also offer compassionate academic solutions to address personal circumstances that are outside of your control. If you have a crisis in your life that interferes with your ability to complete your studies, go and talk with a student counsellor or a physician to find out what your options are. Even if you don't want to withdraw, if what you're going through is big enough to interfere with your studies, then it deserves some attention. If a doctor or counsellor doesn't feel like the right fit for you, remember, you also have your academic advisor to turn to for support and guidance.

Check the fine print in your university's calendar for more information about how withdrawing from a course works on your campus.

Still Stuck? Shake Things Up, Think Like a Genius

If you're still feeling overwhelmed by the magnitude of work ahead, or if you're feeling bored and just wish it could be over, then I'm going to encourage you to shake things up. We tend to fall into unconscious patterns in our everyday tasks but we can challenge that automatic behaviour. Perhaps you take the same route home every day, have predicable morning habits or a "usual seat" in each of your classes. On one level, this is great. Being on autopilot leaves us with less to think about. But the drawback is mental laziness. Studies suggest that too much routine kills a bit of our creative vibe, and this makes it harder to use contextual cues to aid memory while studying.

Todd Siler's *Think Like a Genius* suggests mixing things up.[5] For example, shake up your morning routine:

- Resist checking your texts and head straight for the shower, or have a coffee while looking out the window instead of at your screen.

> **QUICK FACT** 📢
> Mental health issues are a growing concern across the postsecondary sector, so much so that in 2018 the Mental Health Commission of Canada published a set of national standards for the psychological health and safety of postsecondary students. Information about the issues and recommended interventions are available in its report.[6]

- Try putting your pants on with the "other" leg going in first – and then let yourself laugh when you discover how hard it is.
- Eat a different kind of breakfast (or eat breakfast if you normally don't) and try taking a different route to get to your first class.

Taking a different seat in the lecture hall might be too much of a taboo to consider, but for those last classes, I highly recommend it. Most professors use their last class as a review class, and if you're sitting in a new seat, those memories of the review might be anchored in a unique way (with a unique perspective) that will make them easier to recall when you're writing the exam.

I encourage you to throw your entire self into the next few weeks, and shaking up the little things can do just that. Challenging the status quo of life makes our brains more alert, and our memory more open.

Find a Focus and Stay in Motion

Some students find that they need to concentrate on something outside of themselves to break through their wall. They set concrete goals or join a study group where they can give and receive encouragement. Some students say this is the time to get competitive. Fight for a personal best or aim to outperform your nemesis – whatever it takes to get you focused and keep you moving.

Every student needs something different, and as this runner says on Quora, every run (or course) will be different:

Sometimes you are adjusting your pace to reach a target time, sometimes you are preparing for a good pose on the finishing line, sometimes you are trying to encourage a fellow runner to reach his or her target time, sometimes you are repeating the encouraging words you have heard from your fellow runner, sometimes you are just enjoying the run and considering where to run your next one, sometimes you feel like an utter failure, curse the time you decided to take part into the race and solemnly swear never to run again, at least for a while, sometimes.[7]

At the risk of bringing up physics nightmares from high school, Newton's laws of physics hold true for students as much they do for things on wheels. Earlier in this chapter we watched Jenny create a detailed schedule to guide her through to the end of term. Once she got going, she found it easy to stay on track. Bodies in motion tend to stay in motion. And it's also true that bodies at rest tend to stay on the couch.

Students who come into university are already in motion at the macro-level. You're moving towards your adult self; you're developing your skills and discovering your interests. The challenge is to get the motion going at the micro-level – each course, each assignment. When Jenny broke her exam schedule up into mini-deadlines, she was creating motion. That motion continued as she read through her English chapters that night. She was creating momentum again. Even when she wasn't studying, she was thinking about what she'd already done and what was coming next, mulling the topics over in her brain. The motion continued, and you won't be surprised to hear that her assignments were done ahead of schedule. When you hit the wall (as nearly all students do), take the "push" that comes from plotting out your schedule and use that push to put you back in motion. Once you're moving, it will be easier to keep moving. Don't worry about the pace. You don't need to be flying at lightning speed. Slow and steady really does win the race.

Key Messages

☆ Hitting the wall towards the end of the term is normal. Finishing the semester is a gruelling mental battle, especially if this is your first time through.

☆ The biggest obstacle at this time of term is exhaustion.

☆ You've come too far to give up!

☆ Look at your situation. What can we add or remove that would help you succeed?

☆ Withdrawals and deferrals can be considered, but hopefully you won't need them.

☆ Measure the volume, weight, and intensity of each task you have left, then make a game plan based on your time and resources.

☆ Draw out a calendar showing the last few weeks of your term, and plot out your deadlines and other critical dates.

☆ Reassess what you can reasonably fit into this timeframe (work? social time? appointments?). You'll need to put some things off while you get school stuff done.

☆ Build in rewards to help fuel your energy.

☆ Accurate assessment is an antidote to anxiety. Know how to calculate your GPA and do some forecasting to help put your goals into perspective.

☆ If your mind needs to be refreshed – shake things up by doing routine things differently.

RACE-DAY STRATEGIES FOR FINAL EXAMS

What's the best way to approach an exam?
How should I study?
Is it possible to control stress during finals?
How do I get my A-game on for finals?

YOUR FINAL EXAMS will be spread across several race days, and you're going to need some good strategies for managing your stuff, your mind, and your body through this last push. You've been training for this, and good things await you on the other side! When you run a marathon, miles twenty to twenty-four can get pretty dark, but that last mile can be pretty awesome.

Make Sleep a Priority

You won't be surprised to hear that to maximize your exam performance and improve your mental agility, recall, stamina, and focus – the best thing you can do is get a good night's sleep.

FUN FACT
As a young adult, you need about seven or eight hours of continuous sleep to function optimally. If you sleep for fewer than six hours two nights in a row, your attention and reaction times will be three times slower.[1]

Every student knows that sleep is the first thing to go when we feel stressed about how much work there's left to do. Staying up late and then later becomes the norm, even though we "know" it's not great for us. Sleep can also be impaired by worry. When we finally crawl into bed, we can't sleep because our thoughts are tainted by our anxiety about failure, messing up, not hearing the alarm, or forgetting something important.

In these cases, I recommend that you practise visualization strategies to reset your focus on how you want the exam to go. We use visualization techniques a lot in counselling because the unconscious mind can't distinguish between reality and imagination. That means that when you use a visualization strategy, you're giving yourself an experience that you can draw confidence and security from. This is particularly useful in any performance situation, like taking a final exam.

Picture yourself entering the final exam in the best state of mind possible. How do you want to feel? What will your posture be like, or your facial expression? Imagine feeling confident, ready, and eager to write that exam. Close your eyes and try to evoke that feeling as you form a picture in your mind of being confident and ready to write the exam. Imagine yourself working through the questions efficiently with focus and purpose. Imagine finishing with a feeling of accomplishment and satisfaction. Visualization doesn't come easily to everyone, but it's something anyone can learn to do. Try it as a way to boost your power.

Confirm the Date, Time, Location, and Format

This is perhaps a bit obvious to mention, but make sure you double-check the date, time, location, and format of your final exams. Some courses won't have final exams at all; others might have an online test, a take-home exam, or a time-limited, sit-down event. Most likely, your final exams will be of the time-limited variety, with set times and locations in places such as university classrooms or gymnasiums. Some large lectures are divided into smaller groups, and each group writes in separate locations throughout the university. Other institutions combine classes and use larger conference centres or library spaces as test locations. There may be more people in the exam area than you're used to seeing. Expect to see large clocks, timekeepers and exam invigilators, and your instructor, along with a whole lot of tension in the air. Double-check the week of the exam to make sure none of the details have changed.

Open-Book Exams
Some university exams are "open book," meaning you can bring your textbooks in to consult. In these cases, the professor likely isn't concerned about you being able to regurgitate formulas or specific details. These exams tend to be more focused on ideas and application. Make sure you practise creating those kinds of answers in your test-prep time, and pepper your book with sticky notes or tabs to help you find what you need quickly.

Cheat Sheets
Some professors won't set an open-book exam, but they may allow you to bring one sheet of paper in, on which you can list as many ideas or facts as you can fit. Making a great cheat sheet is an art form in and of itself. Often colour-coordinated, handwritten in tiny font, and full of personalized short forms, these sheets have a marvellous way of promoting detailed studying. This might be why so many professors allow them.

A Rock in My Shoe, or How to Ease Test Anxiety
Every semester, I talk with students about ways to take the fear out of tests. It's key to academic success. When you're in that fight-or-flight reaction mode, you can't access your memory well. Your mind goes blank as your heart races, and you begin to get the cold sweats. Test anxiety isn't recognized as a diagnosable disorder because often it has more to do with mindset and preparation than it does with clinical anxiety. Nonetheless, it does cause havoc and can be a real pain during final exams.

QUICK TIP ⚡
If you're interested in seeing sample cheat sheets, you'll find all kinds of examples online, and many sites offer free downloads such as the ones on Andy Friedman's site.[2]

What's great about test anxiety is that it can be treated. It's a real thing. It's like a switch in your brain flips, and you can no longer remember what you've studied. Many students feel frustrated when they wrack their brains during an exam and can't remember "what that thing's called." It's common (and annoying) to remember "the thing" easily once the exam is over.

Test anxiety can be solved by working on your methods:

1. Calm the body (and the mind). To calm the body, counsellors and coaches often teach strategies to help students shut off the fight-or-flight response and re-engage the parasympathetic response (see Chapter 10). They include deep abdominal breathing, positive self-talk, and bringing one's focus back into the here and now (focusing on the place, the sounds, the sensations of the moment). The body can be soothed by tapping our feet on the ground, humming, wrapping ourselves in a blanket, or shaking out the tension in our shoulders.

2. Practise study methods like those we've already reviewed in this book. Test anxiety goes down as test experience goes up – so the best way to get over it is to rehearse the test-taking experience and take as many real tests as you can.

3. Change your attitude – make tests a challenge rather than a threat. Tests can be seen as things that are out to get you or as tools professors use to embarrass their students. The healthier and more useful perspective is to see tests as opportunities to show what you've learned. They're opportunities to help you feel confident that you've absorbed the material, that things have stuck with you through the course, and that your knowledge base is growing. You're on your way to having a degree. By confirming your knowledge through a written exam, you're demonstrating your expertise – to your professor, but more importantly, also to yourself. When tests are seen as opportunities instead of threats, our physiological system calms down and can access more of what we know. It's a self-reinforcing cycle once it gets going.

I almost ended this section without explaining why it's titled "A Rock in My Shoe." This was a creative intervention for test anxiety that I used with a client about eight years ago. She was in our theatre program and had a terrible time writing final exams. She could perform a monologue in front of a live audience, practise love sonnets with strangers, and convey a range of emotions with her movements, but when it came time to write about her understanding of the craft, the history of theatre, or what she had learned in her philosophy class – she froze. Her mind slipped into her long-standing habit of thinking "I can't do this." Her childhood contained many negative messages about her intelligence, and she had internalized a lot of them. She could escape their grip while acting but not during test-taking situations. She felt trapped.

As an intervention, we experimented with deep-breathing exercises and more encouraging self-talk, but it was putting a rock in her shoe that did the trick – something to distract herself from the habit of putting herself down and being afraid. She needed something that would interrupt her thinking and bring her back into the present moment. I don't know if you've ever had a rock in your shoe, but if you have, you know it's hard to ignore.

The annoyance of having a rock in her shoe pulled her attention away from thinking "They're right, I can't do this" and into thinking "What's that in my shoe?" We chose a rock that was smooth enough to not cause significant pain but large enough to be a disturbance. When she felt it, she was flooded with memories of our work together. It reminded her that she could break the test-anxiety cycle. It was enough of a disruption to bring her back to her senses. During the exam, when she felt scared by a question, she rolled her foot onto the rock, and it gave her a soothing reconnection with herself. The intervention helped her feel present in the exam rather than caught up in her worry about it.

She ended up sharing the method with friends, and it became a "thing" in her cohort. I don't know if she used that technique outside of exams but, for her, it literally grounded her attention and helped her break the cycle of test-taking stress.

Final Prep for Personal Best

Drawing on my twenty-plus years of experience working in a university and my ten years of university study before that (!), here are my top suggestions to help you reach your personal best on exam day.

The Night Before

It's finally happening. Final exams are starting and tomorrow you need to be on your A-game. To maximize your performance, put these suggestions into practice on the eve of the exam:

1. Find your wind-down ritual. All professional athletes talk about some kind of evening ritual that allows them to unwind before a big game. Some have superstitious practices (must use a new toothbrush, sleep in tomorrow's socks), but most engage in low-tech relaxation, which allows them a mental break from game prep. This strategy also makes it easier to fall asleep when they crawl into bed.

In the evening before your exam, eat a light dinner and spend time reviewing your materials. Then, about thirty minutes before your head hits your pillow, shut off the computer and your phone and spend the rest of the night in low-tech mode. This is recommended not because phones offer mental distractions (although that's true too) but because the screens stimulate our brains and make it harder to fall asleep. Screens have a quick refresh pattern that stimulates our cortex, and the blue light they emit interferes with our circadian rhythm. Instead – read through your review notes (on paper, not screen) then take a shower. Do some stretches, hug your people, cuddle your pet, and send yourself some positive mental messages.

2. Get your game-day-gear ready to go. Before you turn in, make sure you have everything that you'll need for the exam ready to go. Your bag should be packed and your clothes laid out (although attending a final in your pyjamas is generally acceptable). The goal here is to calm pre-race anxiety as much as possible by making your morning smooth. You don't want to waste time (and fuel anxiety) looking for your notes or your keys.

3. Make a bed cave. You want your bedroom to be dark, cool, and super comfortable. These kinds of environmental cues will trigger the release of melatonin, which will bring your body into a sleep-ready state. Do what you can for sound control and consider using a white-noise app or a fan if you find ambient sound disturbing.

4. Trust your preparation. Professional athletes have an inner coach who streams live positive messages. *You can do this. We've got this. This is what we've been training for.* Trust the work you've put into the entire semester and sleep knowing that you're on track for tomorrow.

FUN FACT

A Stanford sleep study showed that basketball players who extended their sleep to ten hours a night had faster sprint and reaction times and a 9 percent improvement in shooting accuracy (free throws and three-pointers).[3]

The Morning Of

Hopefully you wake up after a good sleep (even with a bit of tossing and turning, excitement and worry), and now it's time to get ready to go. What does a strong morning look like? Should you just get up and run out the door? Consider these strategies shared by many exam-day winners:

1. Eat something easy but amazing in the morning. Even if your exam is early in the morning, prepare your body (and your brain) with some nutrition. This is no regular school day.

2. Clear brain fog. You want your brain to be warmed up by the time you sit down and tackle that first question. You can clear the fog by reviewing your notes, reading a few chapter summaries, or, if you have time, work through a few of your mock questions. This is the equivalent of stretching and warming up before your run. You'll want to hit the exam already revved up.

3. Check that you have your Student ID. Many universities require that you show identification as you enter the room to write the exam. Make sure you have your student card or driver's licence on hand.

4. Bring something personal. Take along something personal or meaningful, something that brings a bit of comfort. It could be a fuzzy pen or a great pair of socks, but bring something that reminds you of your life outside of school. These possessions can act as talismans for race day.

5. Plan to arrive early. Take the stress out of your commute and leave at least twenty minutes earlier than you normally would (even if you're just walking from your res room). If standing outside the examination room causes you stress, go for a walk down the hall or bring a pair of headphones.

6. Enter with confidence. At the beginning of this chapter, we talked about visualization – picturing yourself managing the exam in the best way possible. This is your chance to bring that vision to life. Hold your head high as you walk into that exam room. Enter with a smile. Walk with confidence, ease, and readiness. This is your time to shine.

Ready? Set? Go!
Turn your exam booklets over and start writing.
The moment the exam is handed to you can be terrifying. Write your name down before you forget. It's surprising how many of our

students don't do that! Then, if there's a formula, acronym, memory cue, or a key fact you're worried you'll forget, write that down on the cover.

Then take a deep breath and start the exam.

I know some students who swear by the "going backwards" method – starting with the last question and moving towards the first. They say that the questions worth the most are typically at the end of the exam, and it's best to do those when you're feeling fresh. They also say that some of those later questions help you to answer the earlier ones (especially when the first section is multiple choice).

Regardless of whether you go backwards or forwards through the exam, here's how to approach it:

- If you get stuck on a question – skip it.

- If you feel torn between two answers and don't know which one to choose – circle the question and skip it for now. Or you can make your best guess, but put a circle around it so you can go back and check your work later.

- If you're feeling overwhelmed and don't seem to know the answers to an entire section, skip it altogether and come back to it at the end.

- Make sure you answer all the questions (look on the backside of all the pages or scroll all the way to the bottom of the page).

- Save 15 percent of your allotted time for a reread and review. *Remember, you don't get extra marks for leaving early.* For a three-hour exam, that means you're allocating about a half hour for checking back, catching those missed questions, and reviewing your answers. During your reread and review:

  > Check answer transfers if you're using multiple-choice scan sheets.

  > Look carefully over the questions you've skipped and especially the ones you've circled.

  > Read through the questions worth several marks and make sure you've made several clear points and shown your work.

> For online exams, make sure that you get a "successfully submitted" message before you log out of your account.

When you think you're done, just sit there and breathe for a few minutes. Savour the feeling of accomplishment! Look at how far you've come since that first day on campus. Think about this class and the people you've connected with. If it's your last final, then use this time to look back on some of the highlights from the semester. You're likely finishing first term or first year with some meaningful relationships, some hard-earned knowledge, and a whole lot more confidence in your abilities as a student.

The next term or second year will bring additional challenges and strains but also new and wonderful experiences too. You may wish to investigate majors and minors again, and you'll likely be thinking about practical work experiences in your field. I hope you'll also think about becoming a volunteer at next year's orientation. You have a lot to give to those first-years...and you know their path will be easier if they have a good guide.

STUDENT TIP

I always scan through the exam booklet right away, and it helps me in one of three ways. It either boosts my confidence (I know the answers to these questions!), shows me how to best use my time (that question is going to take me a long time), or alerts me to something I don't know and need to search for. By search for, I mean pay attention to other questions in the exam that might help me solve the one I don't know. That actually happens! One last tip from me – I put little clock icons on some of the exam pages to remind me to look up at the clock. It's easy to get lost in the flow of a question and forget to pace yourself through the exam. Hope it goes well for you! – ORIAH

Key Messages

☆ Final exams will feel like a marathon, or maybe more like an Ironman with different skills needed for each of the events. Prep for them accordingly.

☆ Confirm and double-check all of the details of your final exams: place, date, time, duration, and format.

☆ To maximize your performance and improve your mental agility, make sleep a priority.

☆ Visualization is a powerful intervention for the unconscious mind. If you picture yourself being successful throughout your exams, that image of success will help shape your behaviour.

☆ Test anxiety is not a myth, and there's a method to conquer it. Test anxiety goes down as test experience goes up. Set yourself up for exam practice in every way possible.

☆ Negative self-talk can be disrupted, even by a rock in your shoe.

☆ Treat yourself like the intellectual athlete you are by following game-prep strategies the night before and the morning of the exam.

☆ Prep your brain before you go and set your mind to thrive as you wait for the exam to start.

☆ After it's done, stop yourself from bolting. Before you walk out of that final-final, savour the experience and reflect on your accomplishments.

☆ Consider returning next year as an orientation volunteer and help those new first-year students thrive.

PLANNING FOR SECOND SEMESTER AND SECOND YEAR

What if I failed a course? Now what?
How do I know if this is really what I want to do for my career?

AS THE FIRST semester ends, take some time to recover. After coping with the post-exam flu – a real thing – many students use the break to decompress, catch up on laundry, and spend time with friends.[1] Once you're rested, and before the next term starts, spend some time reflecting on the past four months, on what went well, and what didn't. If you didn't do well, don't despair – we have many ways to help you recover your GPA and go on to a terrific career. This break between semesters is a good time to reflect on your major and your career choice.

Review What's Gone Well

To plan ahead, we must also look back. What's gone well, and how did you make that happen? You managed the workload, navigated the tight turns, and kept up with the pace. You've had experience facing exam stress, writer's block, and simultaneous deadlines. While there have been some bumps along the way, chances are most things have gone well.

How did you do it?

Let me ask you the question I often pose to experienced students: Knowing what you know now, what kind of advice would you give to a new first-year student? (Please know I'd love to hear your suggestions!) I'm curious to know what resources you used and what strategies you found helpful. What was behind your best grade, and how did you organize yourself for successful exams or papers?

Take some time to acknowledge your work and your intentional actions. Good grades don't just happen. They result from effective strategies by people like you.

Face What's Not Gone Well

If you did crash and burn through your first term, please know that this is common – so common in fact that universities have several strategies in place to help you recover. It's important to look at your transcript so you know exactly how your grade point average (GPA) is doing. If it's terrible, don't worry too much – it's fixable.

How do you heal a low GPA? You won't be surprised that I suggest speaking to your academic advisor to create a strategy to get on top of your grades next semester. Repeating a course that you've failed is often wise as a GPA booster, and some courses in the university may be known as "easy A's" (because of the way they are structured or because of the content of the course). Many universities also have undergraduate courses that can improve your study skills and writing prowess, and you might have access to a specialized support group or workshop series to help get you back into good academic standing. I am living proof that it's possible to recover from a low GPA and still go on to graduate school (if that's your wish). Many of us take a year or two to figure out how to do university. Be compassionate with yourself and talk with your advisor about how to best approach next term.

Diving Deeper into Career Decisions

When you find that you have a break in your studies, and time to think about the big picture, I encourage you to reflect on your program and your progress. If you're still caught up in uncertainty about your major and find yourself humming the classic "Should I Stay or Should I Go?" song by The Clash, I recommend you DIVE into the following four questions about career uncertainty.

D – Is It Discomfort or Dislike?

Maybe persisting through something you don't enjoy is admirable in the short term (like a painful lecture or a plate full of broccoli), but in the long term, it's a disaster. You don't want to be stuck in a job you hate. As the old saying goes: If you have a job that you love, then you'll never work a day in your life.

However, as my friend Adam Cave (currently the Chair of International Business and Supply Chain Management at Mount Royal University) reminds me, effective workplaces are full of people who love to work. Work involves effort, and when we put effort into something, that means it's important to us. Let's aim to get you set up with a career that you'll love working hard in.

Of course, at the micro-level of the day-to-day, there will be things that you have to toil through, slog away at, push yourself to get done, or find mundane – and those things will likely always feel like work. But in the big picture, if you love what you're doing most of the time, then you'll find that your efforts are sustainable. You'll be more likely to find that state of flow, where you're working hard but it feels relatively effortless. You won't find much of that if you're stuck in a career you don't like.

If your intuition continues to point you towards change, and you still feel bored, hesitant, or overwhelmed by what you're taking, the next step is to get more information about your options.

Remember Joe, the pigeon-training psychology student? To help him decide what to do, Joe talked with an academic advisor before he went home for the holidays. Two advisors actually – one in psychology and the other in social work. He wanted to understand the differences between these fields and look deeper into his choices. He learned about clinical social work and counselling psychology. He found out that both required graduate studies to do therapy work. Joe learned that social work is more systems-focused with an emphasis on advocacy, policy development, and systemic change, whereas psychology has more of an individual focus that emphasizes science, theory, and practice for human development. These conversations helped him resolve his envy and to feel more secure about his program of choice in the long term. Yes, the students taking the social work program were already learning about client work in second year, but Joe realized that psychology was teaching

THE BENEFITS OF VISION BOARDS

Feeling unmotivated? You might need to reconnect with your long-term reasons for doing your program. Make a vision board of what you're aiming for and keep it by your desk. It will serve as a reminder of what you want to create in your life – what you're working towards.

Your vision board can be large, hand-drawn, and colourful – or you could cut out photos and images from magazines to make your own zine. Rosie's has a house with a swing set in the yard, plane tickets, a photo of a grass-thatched hut by the sea, photos of smiling people, some medical paraphernalia, and a pile of red bricks that she imagines could form the foundation of a school. Even a serious-minded computer professor I know, who "wouldn't be caught dead with a vision board," found comfort from a simple drawing on a sticky note for years.

When you're faced with one of those awful assignments that make you wonder why you're doing this, spend a few moments gazing at that sticky note or full-out vision board and remind yourself about what you're working towards. Doing this might give you more patience to tolerate what you're working on now. There are going to be mucky parts along this journey, but the view on the other side is going to be great.

him theory as a foundation to do a different kind of individual and group work later on.

Joe had to change his expectations. He needed to come to terms with what a psychology undergrad really was and let go of what he thought it should be. Instead of getting upset about what it wasn't, he redirected his efforts. To satisfy his need to work with people, Joe began volunteering at the student peer-support centre in January, which helped him develop listening skills and resource knowledge as he continued to slog away at mastering theory in the classroom.

I – Do I *Need Information about Programs and Careers?*

In Joe's case, he had already narrowed his choice down to two options, but for many students, the possibilities seem endless and overwhelming. If you're feeling uncertain about your program and wonder what else is out there, then you need to make a plan to gather more information. Knowledge about your options will be empowering. While more information is good, it's got to be the right kind of information.

Career fairs and open houses are a solid way to gather information about career possibilities. Open houses showcase programs in the hopes of bringing in new students, and career fairs promote work opportunities and volunteer placements for students. You don't need to be a prospective student to visit an open house: in fact, they're a great way to talk to advisors from multiple departments without having to walk across campus. It's also okay to call or email someone who has a job that looks interesting. Most people like talking about their work and welcome the chance to speak with a young person about their experiences. You can find information on how to do an "informational interview" online.

Guides for specific careers also exist, including this one by Randy Connolly and Faith-Michael Uzoka that I helped to develop for the field of computing: *Computing Careers and Disciplines: A Quick Guide for Prospective Students and Career Advisors* (now in its second edition and available as a free download at www.ceric.ca).[2] Our research showed that students don't understand the difference between information technology, information systems, and computer science, and this book was designed to bring those careers into focus.

Another good resource is the free *Designing YOU* series (designingyou.ca) led by David Finch, and based on the principles of project design. The series includes free podcasts and e-books that guide students to map their careers with intention.[3] In addition to the generic *Designing YOU*, look for specialized books to design careers around various degrees, including English, sports and recreation, journalism, psychology, and information design.

Guidebooks are great, but information sometimes comes along randomly, and you need to be willing to look for it. For Alyssa, the information she needed came from the experiences she was having in her classes but also from meeting another student by chance while lining up for coffee. Talk with students outside your program to see what you might be missing. Take electives in alternative streams, and check out what the person in line beside you is reading.

You also have advisors – information specialists who you can meet with for free. Seeking out direction from an academic advisor is a great idea. Alyssa ended up meeting with an academic advisor in the PR program and was able to switch over to that program in second year, taking many of her marketing credits with her as electives towards this new degree.

If you're not sure what career path you might want, your campus will have many kinds of career advisors to support you. Don't wait until fourth year to talk with your career services centre about work experience options, résumé development, and career planning. Individualized career counselling will also be available, either through your career services centre or through your university counselling centre. Through that process, you'll explore career options and pathways that fit the lifestyle you want.

Investigating job markets will benefit those who worry about what kind of job or salary will be available at the end of the degree. Most provincial governments populate websites with occupational statistics based on actual employment rates, including hiring trends, growth potential, and salary ranges. Rosie found this information helpful because all trends indicated that registered nurses would continue to be in demand. The website she used (alis.alberta. ca) also showed her alternative jobs related to her interests, including respiration therapist, licensed practical nurse, patient advocate, and nursing assistant.

Don't get too wrapped up in job searching right now, though, because the job you're training for might not exist yet. Artificial-intelligence data trainers, Airbnb managers, electric-vehicle power-train engineers, smartphone user-experience designers, and vegan-food marketers have all cropped up as viable careers in the last decade. The gig economy trend is still going strong, and over the course of your career you'll likely have several job titles.[4] Building a repertoire of transferable skills will be your strength.

Regardless of which degree you complete, Canadian statistics indicate that having a degree adds significant power to your lifetime earnings. A study of income data from over 420,000 Canadian graduates from the class of 2015 concluded that postsecondary education was absolutely "worth it" in terms of salary, job satisfaction, and working environment.[5]

IT'S THE DEGREE THAT COUNTS

All seriousness aside, don't take choosing your major too seriously. Some programs are geared towards specific vocations (social work, nursing, accounting, and so on), but most university programs aren't job-focused. Your degree will have lots of content, but mostly you'll be learning how to think critically, be flexible, solve problems, decipher details, and examine the evidence. These transferable soft skills are in high demand across occupations, and they're your gateway into a world of possibilities. For many careers, having a completed degree is what counts, not what you majored in.

V – Is Validation Required?

In addition to getting external information about career possibilities, part of your deep dive into uncertainty should involve checking in with yourself about your motivation for being in school. You came into your program for a reason, and sometimes it's good to pause to ask yourself, *Why did I choose this?* and *Do those reasons still hold?*

For Rosie, her reasons for choosing nursing were grounded in a desire to care for people, to learn about medicine, and to have a profession that could travel with her. She will be the first in her family to graduate with a degree, and she wants to open that door for others. During times of high pressure, she sometimes forgets why she's doing this. She knows she was overreacting when she said she wanted to quit. Her new commitment to herself is to take a break from the pressures of school once in a while, maybe to ski, spend time with friends, or get some sleep. Having put her daily strains into perspective, she knows she'll be able to manage them well. Rosie's reflections over the break validated that she's on the right path, even if it doesn't feel that way every moment of every day.

You may come to a similar conclusion *(I'm in the right program)*, or your reflections about uncertainty may reveal that you really do want to switch out of your major. Giving yourself permission to change your mind can be hard. It might feel like you've failed, let someone down, or done something wrong. Our society values follow-through, and we reward persistence and keeping our word. Sometimes, though, "giving up" one thing opens the door to taking on something else.

If you're worried that changing your mind will let somebody else down, you're not alone. This happened to Alyssa. When she came home to tell her mom about the public relations program, she was met with silence. Her mom had no idea what PR was about, so she thought Alyssa was going sideways. She was angry about wasting money just so her daughter could become some kind of public figure or celebrity. Having your enthusiasm crushed is never a good feeling, but Alyssa decided to go back to her mom equipped with some facts. She brought brochures from the department and an online profile of what a PR professional does. Income data from a government website showed that people in these positions were not typically in danger of being homeless, and the profiles illustrated that marketing and PR were similar but distinct. Alyssa brought the graduation plan she'd made with her advisor, which showed her mom that if the switch was made at the beginning of second year, no time would be lost. Courses could be transferred over as electives. Her mom relaxed as she saw that the ground beneath her daughter was actually solid, and Alyssa's enthusiasm became contagious.

I don't know if your parents will be as easy to sway as Alyssa's mom was, but I bet that they want what's best for you, and I'm sure that having facts will help them understand your enthusiasm. Parents want to guide you towards solid choices that will help you build a good future – a future where you feel happy *and* have a reliable income. Help them to help you by sharing the information that informed your choice.

FUN FACT

Five years after graduation, the median employment income for undergraduate degree holders in Canada was $57,400 (as of 2013).[6]

E – Easy or Good?

As you dive further into uncertainty, you're going to have to ask yourself if you're craving a change because you want something better or just easier. We prefer easy tasks over hard ones. Maybe it was a survival tactic for our species, like getting water from the closest spot or waiting by a snare instead of chasing an animal across the plain.

In today's world, there are many examples where easy is not good. Having cold pizza that's been left on the counter all night for breakfast might be easy, but no one actually thinks it's good. Skipping class is easy, but attending class is better. Growth sometimes requires forgoing the easy in favour of more work or more effort. Indeed, a big part of university's value resides in being forced off the easy path and onto the less easy one. I don't like calling it the hard path, though – it's more like the "good" one.

The good path will challenge you to learn something new. You'll know you're on a good path when you have to work hard to achieve something, and when you get there, you'll feel proud, accomplished, satisfied. Goals that are easy to reach don't mean as much as the ones you have to work for. Getting an easy A is not a bad thing, mind you, but you don't want to have a career that's just easy. You want to find that sweet spot where your next goal is attainable, but only if you stretch for it.

For example, if you have mad math skills, you might coast through a training program and land a bookkeeping job that you could do with your eyes closed. At first, that easy paycheque will seem amazing and carefree. This might seem like enough, but over time, a year or two, you'll likely feel unsatisfied, bored, and in need of something more. You may return to school to pursue a degree in accounting or you may be driven to find more challenge in another part of your life

We're designed to face challenges – facing them is part of what having a good life is all about. But the challenges we take on also have to be in line with our goals and fuelled from within. It takes courage to realize that easy isn't always good.

> **QUICK TIP ⚡**
> For second year, start thinking about ways to study in another country while you're completing your undergraduate degree. Field school experience in Honduras or India could give you international experience, credits towards graduation, and a bank of lifelong memories.

Recap

You don't have to be 100 percent certain all the time. It's okay to progress through your program even if you're not quite sure it's right for you. Keep your eyes open to other possibilities as you continue to attend class, do the readings, and study for exams. Use campus services to help you refocus your uncertainty – academic advising for exploring the possibility of adding a minor, career services for looking at work-experience options, or counselling for exploring alternative career pathways.

About a quarter of students drop out or choose to take a break from university after their first year. Uncertainty is a major reason for this, and it's okay to take that time off to regroup, recover, or make a new plan. Although Stats Canada makes it clear that university graduates have lower rates of unemployment and higher incomes (on average) compared to their less-educated peers, there are thousands of drop-out success stories out there.[7] You don't need a degree to be happy or successful. There are other paths you can take to realize your goals.

If you do choose to finish this degree, remember you can always augment it by adding a concentration, another minor, or a work term; by doing an overseas study program; or by bringing in an after-degree certificate to help you specialize. If the study-abroad option is of interest, stay tuned to your international office's updates. Applications usually open up in the Fall term.

If you choose to switch programs, remember to speak with an academic advisor. Many classes are transferable to several pro-grams, and they'll be able to guide you through those details. If you're looking to switch to another institution, keep your course outlines, and book an appointment with an advisor or recruiter at your destination site.

Sometimes changing your mind means accepting that you've made a wrong choice. That can be humbling. It also means you see yourself as someone who is in the process of figuring things out rather than someone who "already knows it all." This is attractive to employers (believe it or not) – because overconfidence can lead to errors, and cocky people are hard to work with. Expertise is some-thing you absolutely want, but it will take a while to become an "expert." Being able to admit when you've made an error is a mar-ketable quality.

Be the kind of person who can reassess decisions and make new ones based on new data.

Key Messages

☆ As the semester closes, it's important to take the time to reflect on what you've been through. The wisdom you glean from this will guide your success in the semesters ahead.

☆ Career uncertainty is normal – especially among first-year students. It's okay to reassess and change your mind now that you have more experience in university.

☆ If you're questioning your choice of major, have a good rest and do a deep DIVE into your uncertainty.

☆ Is your uncertainty happening because you dislike the program, or is it about your discomfort? Sometimes we have to let go of our unrealistic expectations. You won't love every class, but you may love the program.

☆ Do you need more information about the programs and careers available? Don't get too worried about the job waiting for you at the end of the university rainbow. New jobs are being created all the time, and university is less about training for "a job" and more about training for a career. Don't underestimate the importance of your transferable skills.

☆ Reflect on why you chose this field of study. Are your reasons for choosing this program still valid?

☆ Did you make the current choice because it was easy or because it was good? These are not always the same things.

☆ Consider adding a work term or a summer employment opportunity to explore your interests and options further.

☆ It's okay to progress through your program even if you're not 100 percent sure that it's right for you.

☆ Your academic advisor and your student counsellors are available through the spring and summer months too. Don't be shy about booking an appointment to get some guidance about next semester or next year.

LOOKING FORWARD TO THE SECOND SEASON

AT THE START of this book, I said that first-year university is like that new detective drama everyone's watching. Even before the first episode's done, you have an idea of what's going to happen. Your university experience will also be like that: predictable in general but not quite the same as anyone else's.

Finishing the first semester will feel like you just binge-watched the first 14 episodes of *Your Undergraduate Journey*, Season 1. Over the winter holidays you may feel eager to continue the story, maybe you have been left with a cliffhanger, or perhaps you are ready for a break. Take time to recoup and recover, because come January, you'll be back at it again, deep into the storyline and caught up in the drama of it all.

By the end of April, after the season's finale, you may feel sad that the experience is over, though hopefully content with how it all came together. The conclusion may leave us feeling let down, relieved, or on edge – wondering what's going to happen next. If the season was just mediocre, then we may feel glum, blah, perhaps uncertain about whether we want to tune in next fall. You may be relieved to have a break so you can do other things. You may feel like you want to postpone Season 2, but after a four-month hiatus, you may feel more open to continuing on. If the first season was great, then you're full of anticipation for what's ahead. It may be hard to accept that it will be four months until the new season begins.

So it is with the first year of university. You've been through many episodes, and now the season is over. You've come a long way.

You might find it hard to remember how you felt during orientation – watching that opening sequence and seeing the university set for the very first time. But then you became immersed in the story and took on a starring role in your own postsecondary drama (or was it a thriller, romance, or comedy?). Week after week, the plot unfolded. The unexpected happened, seemingly minor players became pivotal, and your character development was likely profound. You now know that success at university is not based on intelligence. *Everyone* who makes it into university is intelligent – you are too. You know that successful students are engaged with their programs and courses. They attend class, and they take notes. Successful students use study techniques to increase their efficiency and save time. Yes, they use some of that saved time to review their notes, but they also focus on friendships and get involved with campus.

In your second season of undergraduate life, there will be additional bumps and roadblocks, but you now know that there are friends, family, supporters, and services to help.

Looking back across their university career, what do graduates say they wished they had known in their second year of studies? Here are some highlights from some of the alumni at my university:[1]

- Get as involved as you can – clubs, intramurals, orientation, anything. Explore everything that school has to offer.

- You'll meet more people every year, and each year you'll make more friends. You'll be happier! Go to class.

- Never hide – make friends, be fearless.

- If you have to take time off from school, don't stress too much about it. Do try to come back, though.

- Don't settle for a program you don't like. Most employers don't care what your degree was in; it's more about what you experienced as a student. Don't settle for a mediocre relationship either.

- Try to save up before you start second year. Job + School = Hard.

- Look at your honours requirements now so they don't limit your opportunity to excel.

- Try as many different classes as you can.

- Talk to your professors. Ask for help. Your teachers want you to succeed.

- Find the smart kids. They'll help you, and you'll be forever grateful.

- Have fun with everything that comes your way. If you ever get the chance, take a field study program. Go abroad. It will open your eyes so much!

- Add a minor. It makes you stand out from others with the same degree.

- Talk to your advisor!

- Stay focused. Learn, but don't forget to live.

- Keep doing what you're doing. Your first year was a successful learning experience. Second year will be even better.

You now know that you're more capable than you first believed, and you have solid advice that you can pass along to next year's first-year class. If you'd like to share that advice with me, I'd love to hear it. Contact me through my website (drjanetmiller.com).

As the final credits roll and your first season ends, walk the halls and reflect on how far you've come. Those new university shoes are broken in, and next year you're going to feel even more at home in this place. Now is also a great time to put your name forward to volunteer for orientation. It's like watching Season 1 again only without the pressure, and it's a great way to start Season 2 of your university life.

ACKNOWLEDGMENTS

JUST AS YOUR journey through university is supported by friends, family, teachers, and mentors, so it has been with my journey through writing this book. My first thanks, of course, must go to the thousands of students I've sat with over the years. Thank you for allowing me to share in your experiences, to support your struggles, and to celebrate your successes. I have had the best career imaginable because I've had the privilege of working alongside you.

In developing this manuscript, I have had the great fortune of working with a strong publishing team. I will always be grateful that I met Melissa Pitts, director of UBC Press, while attending the Congress of the Humanities and Social Sciences in Vancouver. Melissa's enthusiasm for the press's On Campus imprint was contagious, and her vision fit perfectly with my hopes for this book. Valerie Nair was pivotal in promoting my early prospectus, and Nadine Pedersen, my acquisitions editor, championed this work. Nadine was the best guide I could have asked for to take me through this process. She is the right balance of deadlines and patience, serious critique and wicked humour. I am grateful that the editorial process was guided by the skilful Ann Macklem, my production editor. I admire Ann's project-management skills and her attention to detail. Thank you for identifying my mistakes and helping me to correct them. Thank you for finding sources, listening to my feedback, and making suggestions that significantly improved the quality of this book. Without you, this book would not have reached the shelves. I also had the great pleasure of working with Lesley Erickson, an outstanding editor and publishing specialist. Thanks to her expertise, the writing became smoother and the sequence of chapters reorganized into what I hope you'll agree is a strong narrative focused on the first term. I'd like to also extend my thanks to the rest of the UBC Press team, to those who worked on the book and cover design, indexing, proofreading, marketing, and publicity, including Patricia Buchanan, Laraine Coates, Kerry Kilmartin, Gerilee McBride, and Carmen Tiampo.

Outside of the production process, I have many people to thank and not nearly enough space to fully acknowledge their support, contributions, and input. Sarah Rude tops my list of mentors, helping me sort through the chaos of early ideas, sitting with me to organize my knowledge into chapters, and outlining each one on large, bright sticky notes posted across the walls of my office. She also organized and facilitated the focus group that kicked this process off. Sarah is one of those incredible people who you just can't quite believe you're lucky enough to know. I am in her debt. To the members of that focus group – Brian Arseneault, Kyra Bird, Chula Casey, Jason Droboth, Ploy Ethamma, Zoe Slusar, and Jordan Verhappen, thank you for your input, honesty, and stories. Thank you for telling me that my initial ideas sucked and for supporting me to find the right path leading here to *You @ the U.*

After a very inspiring conversation with my cousin Scott de Koning, who happens to also be a motivational speaker and morale specialist (thank you, Scott!), I made the leap into action by hiring a professional writing coach. That incredible person is Robin van Eck – author, coach, editor, and executive director of the Alexandra Writers' Centre Society. After letting me spread my sticky notes across her long tables, she told me it was time to put them away and start writing. Actual writing. She reviewed my early drafts, quickly banned me from using semicolons, and put a large, red X through the smiley face I left at the end of the Introduction. She taught me how to use words instead of exclamation marks and challenged me to try a bit of dialogue when writing about the aviation class. We laughed a lot and wrote even more. How I miss those afternoons.

Thank you to all the people who shared their thoughts about first year with me, especially those who provided feedback on early drafts of this work. The list is long, but I'd like to give particular thanks to Sarah Armstrong, Katharine Barrette, Miriam Carey, Yasmin Dean, Sonya Flessati, Andrea Heron, Jodi Nickel, Jennifer Pettit, Rea Sauter, and Courtney Warren for reading entire drafts and providing detailed commentaries. Thank you to Brandon Smith for multiple readings and for lending me his expertise, research ideas, patience, and love throughout this project (and this life). Thank you to Cari Ionson, Todd Nickle, Sam Pearson, and Deanna Wiebe for providing feedback on particular sections related to their areas of expertise, to Mirjam Knapik, Kandi McElary, and Mount Royal University for giving me the time and encouragement to write, and to Andrea Phillipson for her leadership through two excellent writing retreats. Thank you to Adam Cave, Andrea Heron, Elizabeth Lourens, Mizuki Oshita, and Patrick Perri for sharing their ideas and experiences. Patrick, thanks for allowing me to share your father's wisdom here to help students navigate through the sharp curves of university life. I also loved hearing about CEGEP experiences from friends across the country, and I appreciated all those who sent me resources, links, and articles to consider.

Being a member of the Canadian Association of College and University Student Services (CACUSS) has been incredibly formative throughout my career, and I am grateful for all of the encouragement and support I've gained through this national community. I am in awe of Jennifer Hamilton (executive director) of that group and appreciated her ideas for reviewers and outreach. To the anonymous reader, please know that your feedback was truly outstanding. Your thoughtful critique has made this work stronger, more practical, and more inclusive. I felt supported by your review, and I am so grateful for the time and effort you put into it, especially given that it all happened during the pandemic. Thank you!

A special shout-out to Kaylene McTavish for her ongoing enthusiasm for all things NSO (New Student Orientation) and for providing me with many ways to stay connected to the incoming cohorts of first-year students. And thank you to Glen Ryland for using early chapters in his undergraduate studies class and for inviting me into the class as a writer-in-residence. What a pleasure to work with Deb Bennett and Michael Sauvé, alongside many classes of first-year students. Karim Dharamsi, thank you for encouraging this connection. Thank you to the host of fantastic friends who supported me through the process of getting this done, including my triad, my book club, Charmène Brewer, Alex Burton, Melisa Centofanti, Diane Gardner-HoFatt, Glenice Grover, Roy Kuhnlein, Betty Ann Lough, Dee Miner, and Tash Reynolds. A very special thank you to Alex Connolly, Ben Connolly, Shira Eisen, Annie Espanola, Eddie Kuhnlein, Robbie Kuhnlein, Kierah Patterson, and Ellie Saunders for their insider information on the undergraduate experience, and their encouragement of this work. And let me top off this list with a thank you to my brother, Chris Browne, for leading the way into university and for having my back through all the ups and downs of this life.

I am fortunate to live with my strongest supporters, and without them, I would most certainly still be at the thinking-of-doing phase rather than the reflecting-on-what-I-have-done phase (this one is much more enjoyable). Thank you Mark for the deep conversations and late-night encouragement, and thank you Hannah for sharing so many practical tips about motivation and time management. I am so grateful that you both have been at my side through this process. Thank you for believing that, of course, I could get this done. Thank you, wonderful Randy Connolly, for loving and supporting me through all of this. I could not ask for a better life partner. You supported the creation of this book from the paper-napkin stage all the way through to choosing the cover. You brought Leo Tolstoy into these pages, the metaphor of the TV drama was yours, and while I found your red-pen edits to be intimidating, each and every one of them strengthened this book. You are a wonderful best friend and mentor. All my love.

Please allow me to finish by acknowledging my deep thanks to Elder Roy Bear Chief for his guidance and support. Thank you for gifting me with many stories and for helping me to listen deeper. I am forever grateful.

A QUICK TOUR OF STUDENT SERVICES

THE FOLLOWING IS a list of typical student services on most Canadian campuses. These services are usually provided at no extra charge (your tuition, student-services fees, or student-association membership fees fund these services). Your university likely also has a variety of online and in-person delivery options. I present this list alphabetically, but some services are offered under a variety of headings.

Please note: Just because it's listed doesn't mean it's available on your campus. Each setting is unique, and services and titles change often. Check your university website (or ask your advisor) for details specific to your campus. As a general rule, if you have a student need, then you'll likely find a student service for it.

In addition to the services listed below, look for stadiums, observatories, outdoor hubs (or bowls), gardens, atriums, museums, greenhouses, ponds, and plazas. Each institution has its own unique set of places and spaces to help you reflect, relax, focus, and socialize. Every one of these services provides learning opportunities outside the classroom, allowing you to connect further with the university's ultimate agenda – higher education.

Academic Advising

Academic advisors are fundamental to your success. Advisors are campus experts on course requirements, registration policies, program options, transferable credits, and elective choices. But they won't simply tell you what to do. Throughout the advising process, you'll explore your educational goals, academic choices, and options to create an undergraduate experience that harnesses your strengths and interests. Each university does advising a little differently. You may find faculty advisors in your program or school, general advisors in a centralized office, or advisors specific to the first-year experience.

Accessibility Services

These services promote barrier-free access in all campus environments, including classrooms, services, and activities. If your university supports the concept of universal design, you can bet these experts have led the initiative. Accessibility services promote inclusion and equity and provide support for students living with a disability. Guided by federal and provincial legislation, these offices advocate for appropriate accommodations and provide targeted support and adaptive technology interventions. If you're entering into postsecondary learning with an individualized program plan (IPP) from high school, a diagnosis of a learning disability, or a diagnosis of a chronic physical or mental health concern, you'll want to talk with an access advisor to organize a plan of support.

Arts Centre

Some institutions have a cultural arts centre that hosts exhibits, performances, events, and workshops. Yours might have studio space, rehearsal halls, or a professional gallery – it's well worth exploring.

Black Students' Alliance

The key objective of this association is to unite and empower Black students on campus. The mandate of these groups is to develop, support, and promote programs that support Black-identified students academically, financially, politically, and socially. These groups create a network of supportive members who contribute to one another's success.

Campus Pub

I'm listing this as a resource not because I want you to use alcohol for coping (you know that's not my hope!) but because it is an important space for socializing and unwinding. Campus pubs often have the best food on campus, and they host local bands, provide a wide range of entertainment, and offer spaces for club activities. They're a good place to schedule a meet-up with a new classmate, so long as you remember to still go to class.

Campus Security or Safe Walk

If you'd like someone to walk with you to your car, residence room, or bus stop, then your campus likely has a program to support you. Most Safe Walk programs are linked to the campus security team and are available 24 hours a day, 365 days a year.

Career Services

This service provides career education, employment support services, and career mentorship opportunities or programs. Career-services experts hope to empower students to feel ready to enter the job world with a well-designed résumé, job-search skills, confidence in the interviewing process, and a well-developed vision for their career plan. They often bring career fairs and volunteer forums to campus, coordinate co-op or work-placement opportunities, and host some kind of job board.

Centre for Innovation, Creation, and Entrepreneurship (Innovation Lab/Makers' Studio)

Many university campuses are integrating innovation labs and maker spaces into their communities to address societal issues. Designed to be interactive and creative spaces that produce new products, initiatives, or insight, these spaces offer students a place where they can expect to be stretched, challenged, and engaged. You'll likely connect with local businesses, industries, and governments, and the work will likely integrate with your university's mission, programs, clubs, and services.

Child Care Centre

This service won't be free, but child care student subsidies may be available. Many universities have an on-site daycare, and most have spaces reserved especially for new students who have child care needs. In addition to child care services, many of these centres also provide resources to support student parents as they navigate student life.

Emergency Financial Aid

Ask at the Student Financial Aid office, the Counselling Centre, or the student union office for information about food bank services and food sustainability supports. Many students struggle with finances through school. Know that there are a lot of on-campus supports to assist you. Common resources include no-interest, short-term student loans, emergency student bursaries, food bank hampers, boxes of produce at reduced rates, grocery cards, and discounted transit vouchers.

English- or French-Language Centres

If you are in the process of learning French or English, if you have to meet a language proficiency program requirement, or if you want to improve your academic writing, you'll find support through these centres. Some universities also offer formal English or French classes for credit and provide opportunities to practise casual conversation skills.

Financial Aid and Awards Office

This office organizes access to student scholarships, grants, bursaries, emergency funding, and other financial support. If you have a student loan, it may be organized through this office (though you likely applied to the government for that support). Many of these offices also offer financial aid (including emergency loans or bursary programs) during times of distress, and they may also offer budgeting support. If you didn't apply for a scholarship this year – please talk with them about applying for next year. Scholarships and bursaries are awarded for academic excellence, and some target specific programs or populations. Ask for details at your university.

First-Year Office/First-Year Experience/Transition Support

All universities have an orientation program to welcome first-year students, but some also have year-round programming. Services may include social events and activities, mentorship programs, links to first-year cohorts, friendly competitions, and off-campus events. Through these offices, you can receive tips for student life, including reminders about when to register for future courses or when to apply for scholarships.

Graduate Students' Society/Graduate Student Services

These supports won't be relevant to you as a first-year undergraduate, but if you have plans to complete a master's or doctoral degree, then these services could offer you some direction and advice.

Health Services

Most campuses host a medical office designed to support current students (and perhaps their families). In addition to support for sexually transmitted infections, these clinics usually offer flu vaccinations, pregnancy counselling, mental health support, and complete physical exams. All health services teams include physicians and nurses, but many also have psychiatric support, mental health specialists, dentists, chiropractors, physiotherapists, massage therapists, or athletic therapists to support your success. Your health supports may also include a pharmacy, naturopathic services, or injury prevention clinic.

Human Rights/Diversity, Equity, and Inclusion

Your university is committed to protecting human rights and will have policies in place to address discrimination and harassment. You have a right not to be excluded, harassed, or otherwise discriminated against based on your race, ancestry, place of origin, colour, ethnic origin, creed, religion, disability, age, marital status, family status, sexual orientation, gender identity, gender expression, or sex. Each university has official procedures for lodging complaints and resolving conflicts. Experts are available to provide training to students, faculty, and staff.

Indigenous Student Services

To improve the student experiences and success of First Nations, Inuit, and Métis students in postsecondary education, Indigenous student centres host cultural events, provide opportunities to connect with Elders, deliver programs to the campus community, and offer a variety of student supports. You may find an Iniskim Centre, a Longhouse, or a First Peoples House on your campus. Whatever the space is called, you'll most certainly find friendly faces, good food, and the opportunity to relax in these centres. The doors are open to all members of the university community, and the staff are friendly experts ready to guide you through any situation.

International Student Services

International students have specific questions and needs, and you can expect your university to have some specialized services to support you. These resources often include academic supports and advising, information on health coverage and immigration, links to on-campus employment opportunities, and social activities to help you meet other students from Canada or abroad.

Intramural Sports

Recreational sporting leagues are open to all students, regardless of skill level. These leagues may have a competitive edge to them, but the focus is mostly on having fun. They are a great way to connect with other students and highly recommended by senior students.

Learning Services

These services go under a variety of names, including the "Learning Skills Centre," "Learning Commons," "Student Learning Services," "Learning Strategists," and the "Academic Success Centre." I don't know what it's called at your university, but I know these services will be on your campus. This group provides workshops, seminars, webinars, and one-on-one professional or peer support to strengthen your academic skills. If you want to enhance your research paper, lab report, math skills, or test-taking skills, this is the place to go. Want to learn more about how to reference citations in a paper? Look no further. Want to be matched with a tutor for a specific course? Ask your learning support office about who's available.

Library Services

The library is the heart of all universities. Smaller universities tend to have one library, while larger universities have many. You'll have access to year-round support from librarians and other experts (research assistants, subject specialists, archivists, and technology-support gurus). In addition to a broad collection of books, music, e-books, films, and other materials, your university library includes a large electronic journal collection that is accessible around the clock. Research guides, support for referencing materials, interlibrary loan requests, and a textbook collection will likely be among the resources you'll find at your university library. Some institutions also offer a selection of board games, laptops, and musical instruments available for loan.

Mature Students' Association

If you're older than the average first-year student (say, between the ages of twenty-five and ninety-five), you may want to seek out connections with other mature students. Some institutions have societies or groups that provide opportunities for social connection or offer targeted support for the multiple demands you're likely facing.

Mental Health

In addition to formal services, including counselling services and health services, your campus may have a mental health strategy or a campus health team. Many universities host peer-support programs designed to engage students in activities that promote mental well-being. Mental health campaigns are common (e.g., Bell Let's Talk) as are websites that provide resources to address mental health concerns or support those living with a mental illness.

Multifaith Centres/Chaplaincy/Spirituality/Centres of Religious Pluralism

Faith centres might be combined into one location or spread across your university campus. Expect to find open spaces for discussion, confidential guidance on personal and spiritual issues, and space for prayer. These centres often support a variety of cultural practices and support students in locating worship communities for different faith traditions.

Off-Campus Housing

This student service is designed to help university students find a place to live off campus. The office is usually staffed by a team knowledgeable about the community and surrounding area, and it's typical to find a housing board that lists available accommodations. This office will likely help you make calls to potential landlords, and they may help you determine the general area you'd like to live in. Off-campus housing teams do not usually do house inspections, and they won't help you negotiate rent, but they will give you information about the Landlord and Tenants Act for your area, along with information on tenants' insurance.

Office of Student Conduct

You might not seek this office out, but it's good to know it's there. This service is generally called on when there's been a violation of the student code of conduct, perhaps a charge of plagiarism or inappropriate behaviour. The office supports students by informing them of their rights as well as their responsibilities.

Ombudsperson/Student Advocacy

The ombudsperson is an impartial support who is there to ensure that all members of the community receive fair and equitable treatment during their time at university. The Student Advocacy office usually helps students to self-advocate by providing support, guidance, training, and knowledge.

On-Campus Student Housing/Residence-Life Programming

When you choose to live on campus in student residence, you're choosing to be part of a community. You'll have personal support, academic support, the convenience of living close to your classes, a commitment to safety, and social programming designed by student leaders (often called resident advisors, dons, or floor coordinators) or permanent residence-life staff. The residence team aims to create and implement programs throughout the year to help guide the academic and personal success of residents.

Physical Fitness and Recreation

In addition to intramural sports programming, your university likely has a place to run, swim, spin, or climb. Your student ID card may give you entry to a wide range of gym facilities, though some institutions charge user fees for lockers, specialized classes, workshops that lead to certification, equipment rentals, or court rentals. Check your campus centre for details.

Queer Spaces/Pride Centre

You're going to find all kinds of queer-positive initiatives on your campus – social, political, and informational support services provided by queer students for queer students. Look for pride centres, queer collectives, LGBTQ2SIA+ services, Pride Parade committees, and gay alliances.

Racialized Students' Collectives

These collectives seek to combat racism and colonialism with and for racialized, Black, and Indigenous students. In addition to advocacy groups that provide social, financial, and academic support, some campuses also host student support groups and services and run anti-oppression programs.

Safe House, Temporary Urgent Housing Support

If you are impacted by a domestic violence situation and in need of urgent support, many universities offer temporary accommodation to support your safety and well-being. Please contact your residence office or your counselling centre to inquire about services on campus and resources available in the community.

Sexual Assault Centre/Sexual Violence Prevention and Response

These centres provide intervention support to survivors of sexual violence, inclusive of all genders, sexualities, and backgrounds. These experts are often linked closely to community services, and in addition to crisis support and intervention, they provide education and training throughout the university. They aim to work towards a future free of sexual violence, and you can expect their support to operate within an anti-oppressive, intersectional, trauma-informed, and person-centred framework.

Sexual Health Resource Centre/Sex-Positive Centres/Sex and Gender Resource Centres

Somewhere on campus, you'll find a student centre that offers nonjudgmental, sex-positive, pro-choice, queer-friendly support, information, and dialogue. Go to these safe places to talk about relationships, sexual health, and sexuality. In addition to free condoms and literature on resources, expect to find knowledgeable staff who are open to your questions or concerns.

Student Counselling

Usually free, and always confidential, these professional services offer personal counselling, crisis-intervention, and career counselling support for students. In addition to individual counselling sessions, expect to find mental health support, workshops, groups, and online resources.

Student Success/Student Retention/Student Leadership

These offices go under a variety of names but all are interested in supporting student success inside and outside of the classroom. Their services include leadership training and conferences, organization of early support services, or head-start initiatives to help you get oriented early. Some universities have an Outstanding Scholars program to prepare students for taking on leadership roles. Others have LEAD programs or leadership training seminars.

Student Union (Association, Society, or Council)

All students are members of the university's student advocacy group, which goes by different names across the country:

- *Student Union* (e.g., Acadia University, Brandon University, Brock University, Concordia University, Lakehead University, Memorial University, Mount Allison University, Thompson Rivers University, University of Manitoba, University of Regina, UPEI)

- *Student Society* (e.g., McGill University, Queen's University, Simon Fraser University, University of Northern BC, University of Victoria)

- *Student Council* (e.g., Bishop's University, First Nations University of Canada, University College of the North, University of Western Ontario)

- *Student Association* (e.g., Saint Mary's University, Trinity Western University, Université du Québec à Montréal, University of Waterloo, University of Winnipeg)

- *Federation* (e.g., York), or *Alliance* (e.g., University of Windsor).

This association (whatever it's called) aims to represent your interests. It provides student-focused services and events and typically operates independently from the university administration. The student body elects student leaders to executive positions, and that group advocates for your collective rights. It aims to represent student interests to the university and government and to add quality to your student life.

Clubs and societies are often hosted under their umbrella, along with many small businesses, food vendors, peer-support centres, and queer-positive spaces. Most have lounge areas and microwave stations, and some even have nap rooms. Often considered the heart of campus life, student associations are often the group organizing concerts and beer halls. They also organize fundraisers, administer student health-benefits plans, and supply students with emergency food or financial support. If you're looking for a sure way to make connections, build friendships, and gain experience for your résumé, this is *the* place to volunteer.

Study Lounges/Study Spaces/Bookable Rooms

As you walk across your campus, you'll see that many areas are designed specifically for your student life. Some spaces are meant to encourage connection with others, with comfortable sofas, ample plug-ins, large open areas, and modular furniture that can be reconfigured to meet the needs of the group. Other spaces will be designated as silent reading rooms; they often include well-lit individual seating stations behind closed doors with space to plug in your laptop and spread out your papers. Many buildings (and especially libraries) have bookable study rooms for group projects or study-group meetings. The best ways to find these spaces? Walk around, or ask a librarian.

U-Pass

If available, a universal transit pass (or U-Pass) offers discounted rates for students using public transit. If a U-Pass isn't available, discounted bus tickets may be. Ask at campus security or your student union office.

Varsity Athletics

Available for elite-level athletes looking to compete provincially or nationally, varsity teams represent excellence in sport and excellence in school spirit. All students are welcome to attend home games during athletic tournaments. They are terrific opportunities to socialize and foster community pride.

Wellness Services

This is a broad umbrella term used to cover counselling services, medical services, illness-prevention initiatives, mental health promotion activities, other health services (e.g., physiotherapy, chiropractic medicine), and health awareness programs (e.g., education about healthy body image or substance use and dependence). You may also find volunteer opportunities within these services, as many wellness centres offer peer-support programs.

Introduction

1   Allen Elkin, *Stress Management for Dummies*, 2nd ed. (Hoboken, NJ: John Wiley and Sons, 2013).

Chapter 1: What to Know before You Go

1   #FungBros, "College Freshmen Mistakes," streamed live on August 28, 2013, YouTube video, https://www.youtube.com/watch?v=STs4Hc7OvOo.

2   Center for Community College Student Engagement, *Even One Semester: Full-Time Enrollment and Student Success* (Austin: University of Texas at Austin, College of Education, Department of Educational Administration, Program in Higher Education Leadership, 2017), 2.

Chapter 2: Moving (Even If You're Not)

1   Government of Canada, *Building on Success: International Educational Strategy, 2019–2024* (Ottawa: Global Affairs, 2019).

2   Mary Dwyer, "These Canadian Universities Have the Most International Students: How Schools Compare for Welcoming Out-of-Province and Foreign Students," *Maclean's*, November 27, 2017, https://www.macleans.ca/education/which-canadian-universities-have-the-most-international-students/.

Chapter 3: Orientation and Welcome

1   Government of Alberta, *Transition Planning Guide – A Career and Education Planning Guide for Students with Disabilities* (Alberta Advanced Education, 2020), https://alis.alberta.ca/tools-and-resources/content/products/transition-planning-guide-a-career-and-education-planning-guide-for-students-with-disabilities/; Regional Assessment and Resource Centre, *Transition Resource Guide for Students with Disabilities: Transition to Post-Secondary Education* (RARC, 2020), https://www.transitionresourceguide.ca/.

2   Ryerson University, Sexual Violence Policy, https://www.ryerson.ca/policies/policy-list/sexual-violence-policy/.

3   Dalhousie University, Sexualized Violence Policy, https://www.dal.ca/dept/hres/sexual-violence/sexualized-violence.html.

4   Blue Seat Studios, "Consent: It's Simple as Tea" (British Voice- Over Version), streamed live on June 12, 2016, YouTube video, https://www.youtube.com/watch?v=u7Nii5w2FaI.

Chapter 4: Early Days on Campus

1   Charles D. Spielberger and Laura Starr, "Curiosity and Exploratory Behavior," in *Motivation: Theory and Research*, ed. Harold F. O'Neil Jr. and Michael Drillings (Hillsdale, NJ: Lawrence Erlbaum Associates, 1994), 221–43; Charles D. Spielberger and Eric C. Reheiser, "Assessment of Emotions: Anxiety, Anger, Depression, and Curiosity," *Applied Psychology: Health and Well-Being* 1, 3 (2009): 271–302.

2   Harlan Cohen, *The Naked Roommate: And 107 Other Issues You Might Run Into in College*, 7th ed. (Naperville, IL: Sourcebooks, 2017).

3   Abraham H. Maslow, "A Theory of Human Motivation," *Psychological Review* 50, 4 (1943): 370–96.

4   Cindy Blackstock, "Revisiting the Breath of Life Theory," *British Journal of Social Work* 49, 4 (2019): 854–59.

Chapter 5: Finding Your Peeps and Settling In

1   Jeffrey Arnett, "Emerging Adulthood: A Theory of Development from the Late Teens through the Twenties," *American Psychologist* 55, 5 (2000): 469–80.

2   Mount Royal University, "First Year Advice from Current MRU Students," videographer Mozz Morrissey, interviewer Janet Miller, streamed live on August 21, 2013, YouTube video, https://www.youtube.com/watch?v=mZY1wnQb-Sw.

3   Ibid.

4   Alena Boczek, Janet Miller, Natasha Reynolds, Mark Keller, and Kathleen O'Reilly, "Investigating the Long-Term Impact of Student Leadership Roles," *Communiqué*, Canadian Association of College and University Student Services (Winter 2017), https://issuu.com/cacuss/docs/communique_march_2017.

Chapter 6: The Crash (a.k.a October, First Grades Back)

1   Janet Miller, "High School to Higher Ed: Supporting Students to Manage Stress," *Conference Proceedings of the 17th Annual Hawaii International Conference on Education (HIEC)*, Honolulu, Hawaii, January 7, 2019, http://hiceducation.org/wp-content/uploads/2019/04/EDU2019.pdf.

2   American College Health Association, *ACHA's National College Health Assessment II: Canadian Reference Group, Executive Summary Spring 2019* (Silver Spring, MD: American College Health Association, 2019).

3   https://www.merriam-webster.com/dictionary/reactive.

4   HAP Balanced Living, "How to Deal with Homesickness in College," blog posting, September 4, 2018, https://www.hap.org/blog/2018/09/homesick-in-college.

5   Katie Reilly, "Record Numbers of College Students Are Seeking Treatment for Depression and Anxiety – But Schools Can't Keep Up," *Time Magazine*, March 19, 2018, https://time.com/5190291/anxiety-depression-college-university-students/.

6   Tom Heyden, "The Adults Who Suffer Extreme Homesickness," *BBC News Service Magazine*, June 5, 2013, https://www.bbc.com/news/magazine-22764986.

7   Carolyn J. Duven, "The Problem with Homesickness: A New Way of Coming Home," PhD diss., Iowa State University, 2018.

8   Jerome Tognoli, "Leaving Home: Homesickness, Place Attachment, and Transition Among Residential College Students," *Journal of College Student Psychotherapy* 18, 1 (2003): 35–48.

9   Annie Grace, "'High' Anxiety: Using Alcohol for Liquid Courage Is a Big Mistake," *Daily News*, July 3, 2016, https://www.nydailynews.com/life-style/high-anxiety-alcohol-liquid-courage-big-mistake-article-1.2697985.

Chapter 7: Maybe I'm Not Smart Enough

1   Young Jung, Ambrose Leung, and Janet Miller, "Do Smart Students Study Harder? An Investigation of Efficient Effort among a Sample of Undergraduate University Students," *Journal of Economics and Economic Education Research* 17, 1 (2016): 25–38.

2   Aaron T. Beck, "Thinking and Depression: Theory and Therapy," *Archives of General Psychiatry* 10, 6 (1964): 561–71.

Chapter 8: Time Machines and How to Use Them

1   Elizabeth Lundin, "How to Take Better Notes: The 6 Best Note-Taking Systems," https://collegeinfogeek.com/how-to-take-notes-in-college/.

2   Sue Shellenbarger, "Toughest Exam Question: What Is the Best Way to Study?," *Wall Street Journal*, October 26, 2011, https://www.wsj.com/articles/SB10001424052970204644504576653004073453880.

3   Janet Miller, Brandon Smith, Don Best, and Laurie Hellsten-Bzovey, "Thinking About Emotional Intelligence as a Predictor of Student Success in Post-Secondary Studies," *The Future of Education, Conference Proceedings* (2013): 811–15.

Chapter 9: Messed Up about Majors

1   National Center for Education Statistics, "Beginning College Students Who Change Their Majors within 3 Years of Enrollment," *Data Point*, US Department of Education, NCES 2018–484, December, 2017, https://nces.ed.gov/pubs2018/2018434.pdf.

2   Janet Miller, Brandon Smith, and Don Best, "Predicting Student Retention Using EQ?" (presentation made at the Canadian Association of College and University Student Services' annual conference, Ryerson University, Toronto, ON, June 2011); Janet Miller, Don Best, and Brandon Smith, "Using Emotional Intelligence, Career Uncertainty and Belongingness to Predict Student Retention in a Canadian University: Lessons Learned and Early Findings from

a Longitudinal Study" (presented at the Canadian Society for the Study of Higher Education annual conference at the Congress of the Humanities and Social Sciences, Waterloo, ON, June 2012); Janet Miller, Brandon Smith, Don Best, and Laurie Hellsten-Bzovey, "Thinking about Emotional Intelligence as a Predictor of Student Success in Post-Secondary Studies," *The Future of Education, Conference Proceedings* (2013): 811–15.

3   Domingo Angeles and Brian Roberts, *Putting Your Liberal Arts Degree to Work*, Career Outlook, US Bureau of Labor Statistics, 2017, https://www.bls.gov/careeroutlook/2017/article/pdf/liberal-arts.pdf.

4   Joshua Kennon, "What Is an Opportunity Cost? Opportunity Costs Explained," *The Balance* (December 22, 2020), https://www.thebalance.com/what-is-opportunity-cost-357200.

Chapter 10: The Sh*t Has Hit the Fan
1   St. Michael's Hospital, "Mindfulness and the Window of Tolerance," https://www.stmichaelshospital.com/pdf/programs/mast/mast-session1.pdf.

Chapter 11: All-Nighters and Late–Late-Nighters
1   Ann Williamson and Anne-Marie Feyer, "Moderate Sleep Deprivation Produces Impairments in Cognitive and Motor Performance Equivalent to Legally Prescribed Levels of Alcohol Intoxication," *Journal of Occupational and Environmental Medicine* 57, 10 (2000): 649–55.

Chapter 12: Managing the Stress and Coping with Outside Distractions
1   Stephen R. Covey, *7 Habits of Highly Effective People* (New York: Free Press, 1989).

2   Tasha Hubbard, "'The Buffaloes Are Gone' or 'Return: Buffalo'? The Relationship of the Buffalo to Indigenous Creative Expression," *Canadian Journal of Native Studies* 1–2 (2009): 65–85.

Chapter 13: End in Sight but Losing Steam
1   Kristen Keim, "6 Strategies to Prevent and Cope with Hitting the Wall," *Skratch Labs*, https://blog.skratchlabs.com/blog/hittingthewall.

2   George Sheehan, *George Sheehan on Running to Win: How to Achieve the Physical, Mental, and Spiritual Victories* (n.p.: Rodale Books, 1992).

3   Veikko Punkka, https://www.quora.com/What-goes-through-your-mind-during-the-last-mile-of-a-marathon.

4   Ibid.

5   Todd Siler, *Think Like a Genius: The Ultimate User's Manual for Your Brain* (n.p.: Bantam Publishers, 1999).

6   Brooke Linden, Samantha Grey, and Heather Stuart, *Scoping Review of Current Literature – Summary: Post-Secondary Student Mental Health* (Ottawa: Mental Health Commission of Canada, 2018), https://www.mentalhealthcommission.ca/sites/default/files/2018–10/Scoping_Review_Post_Secondary_Student_Mental_Health_eng.pdf.

7   Veikko Punkka, https://www.quora.com/What-goes-through-your-mind -during-the-last-mile-of-a-marathon.

Chapter 14: Race-Day Strategies for Final Exams
1   Ryan Skidmore, "8 Ways to Sleep Like a Pro Athlete," Simplifaster (blog), https://simplifaster.com/articles/athlete-sleep-habits/.

2   Andy Friedman, http://web.mit.edu/asf/www/CheatSheetsIndex.html.

3   Cheri D. Mah, Kenneth E. Mah, Eric J. Kezirian, and William C. Dement, "The Effects of Sleep Exhaustion on the Athletic Performance of Collegiate Basketball Players," Sleep 34, 7 (2011): 943–50.

Chapter 15: Planning for Second Semester and Second Year
1   Andrea Anderson, "Why Do I Always Get Sick after Final Exams?" Scienceline Newsletter, January 8, 2007, https://scienceline.org/2007/01/ ask-anderson-finalscough/.

2   Randy Connolly, Janet Miller, and Faith-Michael Uzoka, Computing Careers and Disciplines: A Quick Guide for Prospective Students and Career Advisors, 2nd ed. (Toronto: CERIC, 2020).

3   David Finch and Ray DePaul, Designing YOU: Life beyond Your Grades (Calgary: FDR Publishers, 2016).

4   Gianpiero Petriglieri, Susan J. Ashford, and Amy Wrzesniewski, "Thriving in the Gig Economy," Harvard Business Review (March–April 2018). https://hbr. org/2018/03/thriving-in-the-gig-economy.

5   Alana Reid, Hui (Amy) Chen, and Rebecca Guertin, "Labour Market Outcomes of Postsecondary Graduates, Class of 2015," Statistics Canada, https:// www150.statcan.gc.ca/n1/pub/81-595-m/81-595-m2020002-eng.htm.

6   Statistics Canada, Table 37-10-0200-01, Student Debt of Postsecondary Graduates from All Sources, by Province of Study, Level of Study, Field of Study and Sex, https://www150.statcan.gc.ca/t1/tbl1/en/ tv.action?pid=3710020001.

7   Yuri Ostrovsky and Marc Frenette, "The Cumulative Earnings of Postsecondary Graduates over 20 Years: Results by Field of Study," Economic Insights 11-626-X, 40 (October 2014). https://www150.statcan.gc.ca/n1/pub/11 -626-x/11-626-x2014040-eng.htm.

Conclusion: Looking Forward to the Second Season
1   Kaylene McTavish and Janet Miller, 450 Pieces of Advice from the Class of 2015 (Calgary: Mount Royal University, 2015).

PHOTO: RANDY CONNOLLY

JANET MILLER, PHD, is a university student counsellor and registered psychologist who has devoted her career to student success and mental health. Enthusiastic, warm, and wise, she lives in Calgary, Alberta, where she is a counsellor and professor at Mount Royal University and an adjunct professor at the University of Calgary.